# 10 SUTRAS for SURE-SHOT SUCCESS in EXAMS



Seema Gupta

UNICORN BOOKS

*Publishers*
**UNICORN BOOKS,** New Delhi-110002
*E-mail:* unicornbooks@vsnl.com
*Website:* www.unicornbooks.in • www.kidscorner.in

***Distributors***
**Pustak Mahal**, Delhi
J-3/16, Daryaganj, New Delhi-110002
☎ 23276539, 23272783, 23272784 • *Fax:* 011-23260518
*E-mail:* info@pustakmahal.com • *Website:* www.pustakmahal.com

***London Office***
51, Severn Crescents, Slough, Berkshire, SL 38 UU, England
*E-mail:* pustakmahaluk@pustakmahal.com

***Sales Centre***
10-B, Netaji Subhash Marg, Daryaganj, New Delhi-110002
☎ 23268292, 23268293, 23279900 • *Fax:* 011-23280567
*E-mail:* rapidexdelhi@indiatimes.com

***Branch Offices***
**Bangalore:** ☎ 22234025
*E-mail:* pmblr@sancharnet.in • pustak@sancharnet.in
**Mumbai:** ☎ 22010941
*E-mail:* rapidex@bom5.vsnl.net.in
**Patna:** ☎ 3294193 • *Telefax:* 0612-2302719
*E-mail:* rapidexptn@rediffmail.com
**Hyderabad:** *Telefax:* 040-24737290
*E-mail:* pustakmahalhyd@yahoo.co.in



ISBN 978-81-7806-111-5

**Edition : 2008**



***Printed at :*** Aggarwal Printing Press, Delhi

***Dedicated to***

My daughters Aashima and Ameesha
who are enduring this phase with firm determination
and winning streak
&
To all the students
who have resolved to emerge winners

# Acknowledgements

I would like to take this opportunity to thank a few people who helped me make this dream a reality.

Besides the all-round help and unfailing support extended to me by my husband Mr. A.K. Gupta and my daughters Aashima and Ameesha, I wish to convey my sincere thanks to Mr. Ram Avtar Gupta, Chairman of Unicorn Books. Without his support and encouragement, this book would not have been possible.

I also extend my grateful thanks to Mr. S.K. Roy, Executive Editor of Unicorn Books, for his unfailing help and guidance. It is his faith in my abilities which enabled this book to see the light of day.

**—Seema Gupta**

# Contents

# Preface

**EXAMS ? What a drag !!!!!!!!!!!!**

Each one of us loathes exams because they involve extensive study. Studies take away our freedom and make us slog hard round the clock with barely any time for recreation. Even if we try to take some time off in between the study hours, it is with a guilty feeling. Try spending ten extra minutes in front of the TV during exam time and penetrating eyes from all around seem to send a very piercing message across to you.

*Exams are not hurdles but stepping stones to success.*

Despite so much dedication and so much effort, if you do not get the desired result, no wonder you feel disheartened. However, there are times in life when you fail to meet your own expectations. These are the times when you do not know what hit you. One moment you were so sure of yourself and in the next instance, you are down in the dumps. Your overconfidence may take you unawares and confront you with failure. But ups and downs are part of life, do not let them upset you. Keep innovating. Do not stagnate. Be on the lookout for better ways to do things. Leave your anxiety and tensions aside. There is no time for them. You have goals to achieve.

There is no single formula to be successful in exams. But like in any other game, there are certain rules to study. Some techniques, methods and ways may be implemented to get the best out of you. You must already be using most of these techniques, but there may be some which you might not be aware of.

Here, in these **10 Sutras**, we have tried to compile all these techniques which shall help you in achieving your goal. If you follow these sutras, you will become aware of your destination, know about your abilities, develop various skills which are important during exams and most important of all, you will inculcate study habits which make you a winner each time. Good habits last a lifetime.

*May every word you read in this book be in perfect harmony with your thoughts.*

Another important thing is to maintain a balance. Even the best medicine if taken in excess will harm you, while in moderation even poison is beneficial. So apply all these sutras with caution without solely depending upon any one of them. Miss out on any of these 10 Sutras and you will feel insecure. A positive attitude, a high level of motivation and the desire to put in your best efforts will ensure success for you in exams.

With a winning streak, keep going. There is no reason why you should not excel in exams. Our 10 Sutras are there to guide.

Work hard. Success awaits you. Best of luck from all of us. May God bless you.

**—SEEMA GUPTA**

Sutra 1

# Identifying the Guiding Force

***Let me ask you a question.***

***Do you know why you are studying?***

***Most students do not know the answer.***

***They simply study to go to the next class.***

***They study because they do not want to be labelled uneducated.***

***They study because they want to have a degree to prove they have gone through school and college like all the others.***

> To succeed, we must have goals.

***But this is no goal or guiding force. A major cause of low achievement is having no guiding force in life. Most of the students contend that when they reach the appropriate age, their goal will appear before them. Then they will score. Unfortunately, it never happens this way. Once you begin to study, you should have a goal before you towards which you move gradually. If you have nowhere to go, you will reach just there—NOWHERE!***

***You cannot be successful without a guiding force in life. Those who set out in life with definite***

*goals achieve much more than their friends who have no aim in life.*

*A guiding force keeps our mind ticking and helps it release a success mechanism. This success mechanism attracts individuals and circumstances that are in harmony with the goals before us. Suppose you decide to pursue an undergraduate course in Engineering from a good university. It is a burning desire in your mind. It is the guiding force for you. You not only study hard for getting good grades, you also collect all the information about it gradually. You find out the details about the universities offering this course, their fee structure, the admission requirements, scholarships available and so on. To go a step ahead, you may even find out about the possibilities of employment during and after the completion of this course. If the guiding force were not there, you would not have taken pains to collect all this information. How many of your classmates know all these details?*

*So you must remember that to succeed you should have a goal as a guiding force. Keep reminding yourself of your goal everyday. If you are determined, then nothing can stop you from achieving your aim in life.*

> Our life is what our thoughts make it.

# Choosing an ambitious track

***'Abhishek, what do you want to become when you grow up?'***

***This is a question Abhishek has been asked umpteen number of times right from his childhood. Abhishek is studying in class X now and he wants to be a pilot. But he knows what his answer should be—it has to be a good profession which his parents approve of. Through experience, he knows what is expected of him. So he utters the usual words 'Uncle, I want to be a doctor.' The answer keeps his parents happy, that their son is going on the right track. But is he ... really?***

You cannot lie to yourself. You must be sure about your ambition in life and make sure that others know about it too. An ambition gives you a reason to move ahead. It motivates you to study harder.

Ambition acts as the guiding force in your life. It attracts you like a magnet. The more you think about it, the more you feel fascinated with it. This fascination of achieving what you really fancy motivates you further to make positive changes in your life.

*Do not falter. Hold on to your ambition consistently.*

Having an ambition in life fills you with an untapped source of energy and enthusiasm. If you look at the practical aspect of being ambitious, then you will realise that your ultimate goal in life is to have a lucrative career. You are studying for a good career. So besides this reason, if you have an interesting raison d'être to study, you will be all the more determined in your efforts. It will be like having your cake and being able to eat it too.

### Be practical

- Be in positive frame of mind
- Reframe your ambition today
- Aim for something which you enjoy
- Be practical in your approach

Let's go back to Abhishek's case. He wants to be a pilot. To begin with, he must convey his choice of career to his parents. Their approval is very important for him to move ahead. Next, he can join an adventure club in his school and learn adventure sports like rappling, paratrooping etc. As soon as he is eligible, he may join the amateurs' club of pilots who train young students in flying the aircraft.

*Plan to achieve your ambition.*

The fact that you are closer and surer of your ambition gives you a new confidence and assures you that you really are on an ambitious track.

## Let's grill you

**Answer these six questions and check how ambitious you are.**

***Marking key***

Give yourself (2) marks for each 'Right' answer and a (0) for each 'Wrong' answer.

| | | **Marks** |
|---|---|---|
| 1. You never get discouraged by people who mock at you when you share your ambition with them. | Right/Wrong | ☐ |
| 2. You never lose track of your ambition. It is always the driving force in pursuing your studies. | Right/Wrong | ☐ |
| 3. You feel you have the determination to achieve success in your dream ambition. | Right/Wrong | ☐ |
| 4. Your career goals are practical and easily approachable. Others also agree with you. | Right/Wrong | ☐ |
| 5. In pursuing your ambition, you lose track of time. | Right/Wrong | ☐ |
| 6. You dare to dream of changing the destiny of the world. | Right/Wrong | ☐ |
| | | ☐ |

### *Interpretation*

- **Scores 6-12** : You are an ambitious person. You possess the guts to pursue your dreams. You have it in you. So go ahead and aim for the zenith — it's worth the daring. You are sure to get a good rank in exams, if you keep on the right track.
- **Scores 0-4** : You seem to be one among that group which would settle for whatever they get and then crib about their misfortune and lost luck. To excel in exams, you need to learn to be more ambitious than this.

### *Just Chill*

Write down your future plans on a piece of paper as to what you really want in life. Put it away for a while. But review it every now and then.

Are you on track?!

# Discovering hidden potential

***Ruchika was an average student. She wanted to do something substantial in life but she could not pinpoint as to what her ambition was. She enjoyed drawing and had the knack of copying objects on paper. But colouring them was a tedious task for her. So drawing classes were fun but painting classes were bothersome. One day, her uncle came over. He was discussing the design of his new bungalow with her father. He was trying to draw it on paper but it was not clear. Ruchika was listening to him. She offered to help. Within minutes, she managed to draw a clear sketch of her uncle's dream house. This not only impressed her uncle immensely, it also showed her the path to success. She had discovered her hidden potential. She opted for Engineering Drawing together with Science stream in class XI. She was on her way to become an architect.***

*You have it in you. All you need to do is explore it.*

The longest journey begins with a single step. This first step is very crucial. It shows you the path to success. When you look at Einstein, Bill Gates, Stephen Hawking and their likes, you say to yourself—they are the chosen ones. They are gifted people, that is why they have been able to achieve so much in life. Before you form opinions remember one thing, each one of us is gifted in one way or the other. All that remains to bring out that hidden potential is a keen observation and an eye for talent. And who else could do it better than you. You are your best judge and your best critic too. The more you know about yourself, the better your performance will be.

*For most of the walls that hold us back exist only in our minds.*

Successful students have an inquisitive mind. Apply your inquisitiveness to recognise your hidden potential. This will make you confident of your ability. Once you are sure of what you want to do, you will find yourself genuinely interested in your work. You will be an eager learner and not the yawning types who adorn the back benches in the classroom.

By discovering your hidden potential, you will develop interest in your subject. And a high level of interest in the subject is very important to excel in it. Believe me, this will change your entire career graph.

## Let's grill you

**Answer these questions in 'Yes' or 'No'.**

| | | |
|---|---|---|
| 1. | Have you ever tried to do something different from the usual? | Yes/No |
| 2. | Do you grab the opportunity to learn something? | Yes/No |
| 3. | Do you respect the feedback on your abilities from your peers and family? | Yes/No |
| 4. | You choose a subject because you are good at it and not just because your best friend wants you to do it. | Yes/No |
| 5. | You know that you have some hidden potential but you are not able to bring it out in the open for fear of rejection from others. | Yes/No |

### *Interpretation*

- If all or most of your answers are 'Yes', then you have the power to recognise your hidden potential. Do not hesitate in bringing it out in the open. Remember, the world cheers the achievers and follows the leaders.
- If all or most of your answers are 'No', then you have a long way to go. You should analyse your capabilities and recognise your potential.

### *Just Chill*

Allow yourself dream time. Return to this world refreshed and renewed.

# Goal-setting

***Rajiv opted for Commerce stream in class XI. He thought of many career options but was still undecided. He found studies rather boring. One day, he was playing a football match with his friends. A small boy was watching them from a distance. During the break when both the teams were relaxing, the boy came up to Rajiv and asked him, 'Why are you all running after that big ball?'***

***Rajiv smiled and replied, 'Because that is how the game of football is played.'***

***'But why are you playing it?' asked the boy, curiously.***

***'Because we enjoy it,' Rajiv replied.***

***'And what will you get after playing it?' asked the boy.***

***'We will win the game. That is our goal,' Rajiv explained.***

***The boy smiled and went away. This conversation set Rajiv thinking. If winning the match was their goal in the game then what was his goal in life. He, then, realised the importance of a goal and that without a destination, a journey was incomplete. After much contemplation, he decided to pursue a course in Chartered Accountancy. Now that he had a goal, he found his studies much more interesting.***

We need goals because they tell us where we must go. It is a simple fact that unless we know where to go, we cannot reach there. The moment we accept a goal in our mind, we start thinking about it. In the process, our brain releases a success mechanism. Which further attracts individuals and circumstances that are in harmony with the goals before us.

A goal is a dream with a deadline. Working without a goal is like groping in the dark.

Goals must be challenging, achievable, flexible and time bound.

A goal is best achieved when split in parts. Set your major goal first and then set the smaller goals which shall lead you to your main goal. A Science student who wants to pursue Engineering from IIT should first focus on getting an aggregate of 60% or above in the class XII Board exams to be eligible for the entrance test. The next goal should be cracking the JEE i.e. the Joint Entrance Exam. As you learn to cover the distance step by step, long stretches will be covered without much fatigue.

Such is the power of setting a goal.

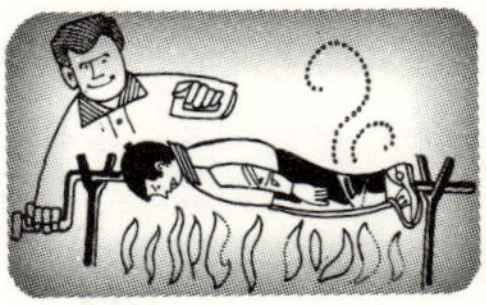

## Let's grill you

**Answer these questions by choosing the correct answer.**

### *Marking key*

Give (2) marks to each 'Yes' answer and (1) mark to each 'No' answer.

| | | Marks |
|---|---|---|
| 1. You always feel a burning desire whenever you think of your goal. | Yes/No | ☐ |
| 2. You have always been a disciplined person. | Yes/No | ☐ |
| 3. Whenever a programme on career guidance is aired on the television, you watch it carefully. | Yes/No | ☐ |
| 4. You prefer to keep your goals simple and realistic. | Yes/No | ☐ |
| 5. You can imagine yourself as twenty years from today and you work towards achieving that dream. | Yes/No | ☐ |
| | | ☐ |

### *Interpretation*

- **Scores 1-5 :** You lack the enthusiasm for setting a goal for yourself. You must realise the importance of goal-setting and try to make more efforts towards it. This is the first step towards achieving success in your academics.

- **Scores 6-10 :** You are well-disciplined and focussed. You are clear in your mind about your goals and that is what helps you excel in exams. You are aware of each step in your path to progress and you are keen on taking them with expertise. Good luck to you.

***Just Chill***

Set a six-month rule while clearing your room. Bag up all the things you don't use but cannot bear to throw away. Put this bag away in a cupboard and wait for six months. If you don't need any of it for six months then you don't really need it. Discard it.

# What motivates you

***Sugandhi's mother worked for an NGO. She went to charitable hospitals to talk to the terminally ill patients in order to cheer them up. On one such visit, Sugandhi accompanied her mother. That day, they visited the paediatric cancer patients' ward. Sugandhi was very much moved on seeing the plight of such small helpless children who seemed to be writhing in pain. They were so small, yet suffering so much. Sugandhi felt sorry for them. Almost all of them were much younger to her. While coming back from the hospital, she asked her mother if there was some way she could help those children. Her mother replied, 'At this stage, there is little you can do. But you can become a doctor and treat many more such patients with love and care. This will be your best gift, not just for these kids but to the society as a whole.' The suggestion motivated Sugandhi. She worked hard in her studies. It was like an invisible force driving her towards her goal. The burning desire to help the sick and needy became the motivating factor in her life. This also helped her set her eyes on her aim and soon she was sailing smoothly towards her goal.***

*If you don't have dreams, they can't come true.*

Motivation is a strong driving force. To motivate means to provide one with a motive to achieve something. At this stage, what could be a better motive than to excel in exams? With your goals set high and your motive clear in mind, where is the room for failure? Success is one of the greatest motivators. Each success will take you a step further to yet another success. With each success, the motivation grows and you will find yourself more enthusiastic, lively and involved, besides developing an absorbing interest in studies.

*Keep yourself in a high level of motivation – always.*

Dedicated work brings appreciation and praise which is extremely motivating. But the greatest source of motivation is being in harmony with your own self.

A fair balance of work, pleasure and rest is relaxing but what one person finds motivating may not be so for another. Individual choices vary. So discover what motivates you best. Create an atmosphere that makes you feel motivated to achieve the goals you have set for yourself.

## Let's grill you

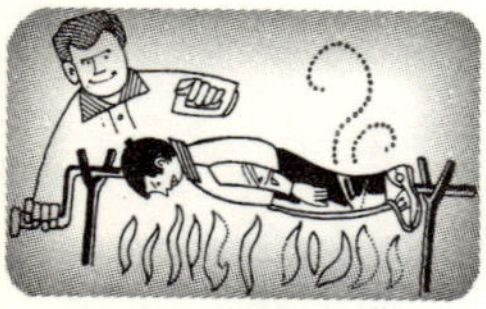

**To assess your level of motivation, answer these questions by choosing the choice you find most suitable.**

### *Marking key*

Give (5) marks to each 'a' answer and (10) marks to each 'b' answer.

| | | **Marks** |
|---|---|---|
| 1. When you wake up in the morning, the first thought that comes to your mind is—<br>a) what shall I do today<br>b) I will work according to my preset time-table. | a/b | ☐ |
| 2. If you are not able to complete a day's time-table, then you—<br>a) forget about it and start afresh the next day.<br>b) squeeze some time out from next day's schedule to fit in what was left on the previous day. | a/b | ☐ |
| 3. You are mostly surrounded by—<br>a) friends who indulge you in fun and frolic.<br>b) friends who understand your need to study and do not disturb you at such times. | a/b | ☐ |
| 4. Praise and appreciation of your hard work motivates you to—<br>a) go out and enjoy as much as you can since you have earned it. | a/b | ☐ |

b) work harder to achieve your goal.

5. For you, motivation is— a/b

a) a bully which forces you to study.

b) a reason to excel in studies.

### *Interpretation*

- **Scores 25-35 :** You are a fun-loving person. You do not take studies seriously. There is lack of motivation in your life. It is quite likely that you do not even have a set goal in life. It is not too late. You must understand that if you wish to excel in exams and achieve your goals, then you must have some motivating factor in life. Make a list of things that motivate you in life and work on them.
- **Scores 40-50 :** Motivation is what drives you ahead. You are in harmony with your inner self. You have all the right ingredients to excel in exams. Read on further and learn more tips on how to excel in exams.

### *Just Chill*

Whenever you sit down to study, speak aloud "I AM STUDYING' and begin your work.

This will become your motivating factor.

Sutra 2

# Arjuna's Dedication

***In the Mahabharata, Dronacharya was the guru of the Kauravas and the Pandavas. He taught them archery. Arjuna, whose aim was perfect, was his favourite student. Once Dronacharya wished to test their skill. He set a bird atop a tree. Before they took aim, he asked them what they saw. Each had a different answer. Someone said that he saw the sky, another said that he saw the tree, yet another saw the bird. When it was Arjuna's turn to take aim, he replied, 'Guruji, I can see only the bird's eye.' His reply pleased Dronacharya immensely, because that's the kind of dedication he was looking for in his perfect student.***

And that is the kind of dedication you need to excel in exams. Concentration is the key to dedication. You cannot do two things at a time. When you split your attention, you cut your brainpower into half. If you have a healthy brain and right attitude, then you can concentrate well. To be able to do so is half the battle won. Concentration is the result of will-power. When you make an effort to concentrate, your brain is stimulated. You are able to focus your mind on your studies without getting distracted by other things. This kind of dedication will take you places.

# Aiming for the bird's eye

***Hansa was a good student. She had an ambition in life. She wanted to become a doctor. So she chose Science stream in standard XI. But she took Mathematics along with Biology on the advice of her parents with a view that in case she was not able to clear the medical entrance tests, then she could opt for Engineering and other related fields. Now studies demanded more of her time. She wanted to focus on preparing for her medical entrance tests but Mathematics being a very time-consuming subject, she could not concentrate on other subjects that well. It was not one of her strong subjects either. She felt exhausted all the time and soon she became disillusioned about her goal in life.***

When you wake up in the morning, do you ever feel elated for having come another day nearer to your goal? I would again emphasise on the fact that you have to have a goal in mind to excel in exams. Unfortunately, all our choices are guided by circumstances rather than our own decisions. But if your journey is not desirable and the road is not clear, then how will you be motivated to move fast on the path.

*Be a student, remain a student, with a focussed mind.*

Reframe your ambition today and aim to be the best. Your job does not end after setting the goal. This is just the beginning. Always keep your goal and your ambition in mind. Accordingly, consider your strengths and weaknesses. Also consider the resources at hand. Now work on your weaknesses while strengthening your strengths further. A time frame must be adopted and regular evaluation of the progress must be made.

### Raring to go

- Once you have set your eyes upon your goal, do not let it disappear.

- Do not change your mind frequently. You will lose confidence in your abilities.
- Set goals for the current year and note down what you wish to achieve.
- Break the annual goal into half-yearly, quarterly and monthly goals.
- Work on the basis of daily goals set every morning.
- Not for a moment should you waver from your set standards.
- Your aim should be to hit the bird's eye. Do not see the bird, only look at the bird's eye.

*Obstacles are those frightful things you see when you take your eyes off your goal.*

## Let's grill you

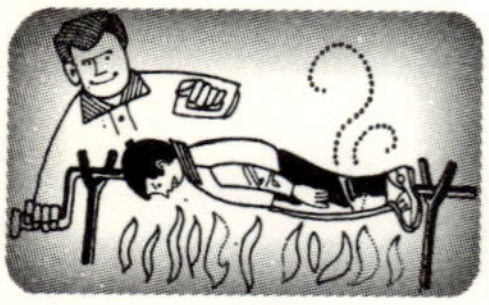

**'Tick' (✓) the points you agree with and 'Cross' (×) the ones you do not agree with.**

***Marking key***

Give (2) points to each 'Tick' and (1) point to each 'Cross'.

| | Marks |
|---|---|
| 1. Most people work without goals, so can I. | ☐ |
| 2. There is lots of time ahead to study, let's enjoy a bit for now. | ☐ |
| 3. Goals should be flexible. | ☐ |
| 4. Once our aim is set, it should be forgotten. | ☐ |
| 5. We shall never discuss our aim with others. | ☐ |
| | ☐ |

***Interpretation***

- If your score falls between 8–10, then you may have scored more marks in this grilling but you do not qualify to replace the *Mahabharata's* Arjuna, because you lack his dedication. You need to focus more on your goal to achieve success in life.

- If your score falls between 5-7, you have the dedication, aptitude and inclination for achieving your goal. You must work towards it with devotion, and soon success will be at your feet.

***Just Chill***

Go out and enjoy yourself.

It should be fun and laughter just for you.

It should be your OWN time.

Soon you will feel happy, uplifted, refreshed.

# Begin your learning process

***When an infant is born, he learns to secure his requirements of food and security instinctively. The deliberate learning process begins when a child is a few months old. The parents speak a few words which the baby learns through repetition. Sound plays an important role in the learning process.***

***A little later, the child begins to learn by copying the actions of his parents. Picking up a spoon to eat or holding a glass to drink or even picking up a small mug to take a bath are all examples of learning through action. Repetitive actions are stored in the child's subconscious mind. Over a period of time, these activities become a part of an individual. That is why activities like eating food and cleaning one's teeth need not be supervised. The child does them automatically.***

***Then the child begins to learn through coordination of activities like learning to swim and cycling.***

***In school, the child uses all these learning processes. He is also taught learning through logic. It is important because now he begins to reason. In this way, the learning process grows gradually.***

*We gain knowledge and imbibe skills through learning.*

With an increase in the scope of studies, we are lucky to have a wider choice of subjects. You may excel in subjects you like and barely pass in the ones you do not like. This clearly indicates that your interest in a subject is directly proportionate to excelling in it. So choose the subjects you enjoy. There are some factors which influence our individual preference for a subject—

- A good teacher
- Earlier achievements
- Appreciation

Another important aspect of learning is that our receptivity to knowledge varies with exposure to information. Let's take an example of a lecture—

- You heard the lecture and want to recall it later. You can do no more than one-tenth of it.
- If you noted the points during the lecture, then the receptivity may improve to one-fourth.
- If you developed these points into notes in greater details on reaching home, your receptivity will be an all-time high.
- The best would be if you put this information to practical use.
- Teaching a similar topic to your friends would refresh your memory and your learning process is complete.

*Life consists not in holding good cards but in playing those you hold, well.*

No two individuals are alike. Their grasp of a subject also varies. So it is important that you look back upon your formative years and understand how the knowledge was imparted. There is always scope for improvement.

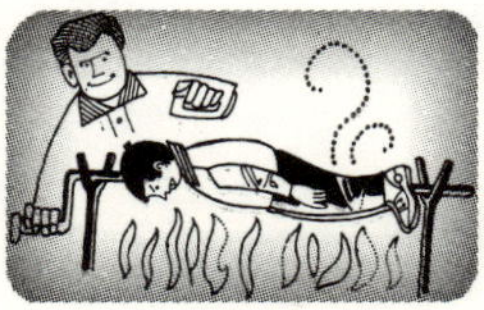

## Let's grill you

**Mark your choice by ticking in any of the columns.**

### *Marking key*

Give (2) marks to a 'Right' answer, (1) mark to 'Maybe' and no marks to a 'Wrong' answer.

| | |
|---|---|
| 1. Learning can add new dimensions to your personality. | Right/Wrong/Maybe |
| 2. To surge ahead you must be sure about your learning responses. | Right/Wrong/Maybe |
| 3. Learning gradually becomes selective. | Right/Wrong/Maybe |
| 4. All individuals develop a personal pattern of learning. | Right/Wrong/Maybe |

5. Learning is controlled by the subconscious mind. Right/Wrong/Maybe

### *Interpretation*

- **Scores 0 :** You are asleep. This is a wake-up call for you.
- **Scores 1-5 :** You do not give much thought to the learning process. Learning may be a part of your growing up years but you do not consider it very important. However, to excel in exams, you need to change your perceptive and accept its importance.
- **Scores 6-10 :** You acknowledge the importance of the learning process. You are aware that learning comes from knowing the 'who, what, where, when, why and how' of a thing.

### *Just Chill*

Laughter is one of the best stress relievers. It relaxes you.

So go ahead—

- Watch a funny film.
- Read a comic or funny story.
- Enjoy a comedy show.
- Get friends round for a good old giggle.
- Take a chill pill.

# Be a voracious reader

***Ravi and Subodh were classmates. While Ravi was a voracious reader who loved to read good books in his spare time, Subodh hardly ever touched any book other than his course books. After they passed their XIIth standard, it was time to appear for entrance tests for different courses. Subodh was surprised to find that almost all the tests had one paper of English language or Aptitude test. Ravi found it easy to sail through these papers because he had acquired a good vocabulary and had a good perception of general awareness because of his reading habits. Subodh, on the other hand, had a tough time preparing for these papers also in addition to his own subjects.***

*Books are one's best friends.*

The best thinkers and idea generators are voracious readers. Unfortunately, most people are poor readers. They are not even inclined to read the newspaper. This lack of interest in reading clearly reflects upon the youth, who only read school and college textbooks. They forget that all progress depends upon development of new knowledge and its use. There is no better way of acquiring knowledge than through books. So if you do not want to be left behind in life, you must read, read and read. There is no end to learning. The more you have it, the more you want it.

*Readers are leaders.*

When you read, you are feeding your brain. Just like people with a conscious food diet enjoy good health, similarly, by reading good literature, classics, autobiographies, self-help books etc. will help you share thoughts with some great thinkers and philosophers. Do not read trash—like romances, cheap fiction, film gossip. Reading good books is essential for an overall knowledge base.

*If you are headed in the opposite direction, God allows U turns.*

All reading material does not deserve similar attention and time. You cannot read a newspaper word by word. But at the same time, you cannot read your textbook like a newspaper by leaving bits of text in between. So, have a balanced reading habit.

**Read efficiently**

- In your spare time, read as many good books as you can lay your hands on.
- Read your textbooks word by word.
- Try to synchronise your reading speed and assimilation power.
- Have wider eye span. Read many words at a time.
- Look for key words, phrases and ideas. They will save you time in understanding the text.
- Read mentally, not verbally. Lip movement reduces reading speed.
- Try to understand what the author is writing. Do not confuse it with your opinion.

## Let's grill you

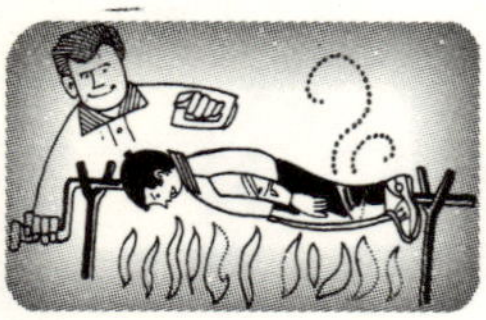

**Let's check your reading skills. Answer these statements by ticking one of the options.**

1. I am so fond of reading that I read anything that I lay my hands on. Yes/No
2. I always read with a purpose in mind. Yes/No
3. I open a book with much enthusiasm, but most of the time I leave it half way through. Yes/No
4. For easy comprehension I try to understand how the book is structured, taking into account the author's style of writing, illustrations and language. Yes/No
5. I find reading a waste of time, money and energy. Yes/No

6. I read in such a way that I can learn more in less time while not missing out on any of the facts. Yes/No

### *Interpretation*

- If your answer for 2, 4, and 6 is 'Yes' and for 1, 3 and 5 is 'No', then you possess good reading skills. You are aware that the purpose of reading a book is to learn and you know how to put your books to the best use. You are a voracious reader.
- If your answers are in contrast to the marking given above, then you certainly need to look into your reading habit. Do not forget that efficient reading can greatly improve the performance of every student.

### *Just Chill*

Plan to be in bed before 10.00 p.m. atleast twice a week. Read a good book for 15 minutes and be asleep by 10.15 p.m.

A good night's sleep will replenish your energy and you will wake up feeling revived and energised.

# Proficiency in writing

***Shashank was an average student. He never scored more than average marks. Everyone was surprised when he scored a good rank in the National Level Science Talent Search Exam (NTSE) in class XI. On analysing, Shashank realised that he scored in the paper because it was an objective type paper. Shashank's concepts were clear but he lacked the writing skills, that is why he never got good marks in subjective type papers. He shared his problem with his teacher, who gave him tips on how to improve his writing skills.***

Reading is one-way traffic while writing is two-way traffic which includes both reading and writing. The best way of studying is by reading and then writing the notes. There is no oral exam. So, you may be a great speaker, you may be a voracious reader, but ultimately, you HAVE to write your answers.

You cannot cram every subject. Take Physics or Mathematics for instance, you cannot learn them—they need to be practised. Commit the mistake of learning Mathematics and your brain will very conveniently forget sums. Answer me this simple question, if you are going to play badminton, will you practise chess? That's the logic behind writing, instead of oral revision.

*Writing requires more attention than reading.*

Do not write isolated answers, solve model papers instead. You may feel tired initially but slowly you will get used to writing for three hours at a stretch.

Writing creates a reference. You can always go back and refer to it if you have put down all that you have learnt, on paper. Writing is the best way to maintain your notes. Notes not only refresh your memory but they also keep the burden of storing lots of mugged up data off your mind.

# Let's grill you

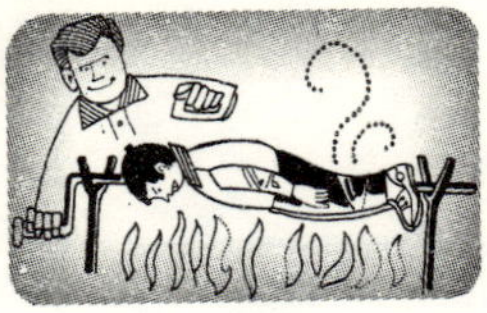

**What is your attitude towards making notes? Tick the right choice.**

1. I **always/never** make notes of whatever I study.
2. The notes I make are **clear and understandable/cannot be** read again.
3. I find notes **effective/ineffective** in preparing for exams.
4. Whenever I make notes, I **do/do not** mind lending them to others.
5. I prefer **written/oral** revision.

*Handwriting is an art open to any amateur, for the delight he gets from it himself and the pleasure he gives to others.*

***Interpretation***

- If you mostly agree with the first choice, then you are on the right track. You not only know how to make good notes, you also know their value. You know that making notes helps in making the subject a part of long term memory. So keep it up.
- If you mostly agree with the second choice, then you need to take a new look on making notes. You can increase your success manifold by making good study notes.

***Just Chill***

Note your day's experiences in a diary each night before you tuck in.

# Improving concentration

***Raja's cousin, Ravindra, lived in Bangalore. Once, Raja went to Bangalore during his summer vacations. Ravindra's exams were not yet over. One day, Raja saw him solving sums, then ten minutes later he saw him doing an English model test paper of three hours. But within half an hour he found Ravindra switching to Physics. This aroused Raja's curiousity. He asked Ravindra why was he hopping from one subject to another. Ravindra said that when he got bored with a subject, he left it there and picked up another subject till he got bored with that also. Raja asked him how was he faring in his exams. Ravindra sheepishly told him that he got average marks in all the subjects. Raja told him that the problem was not his level of intelligence but his lack of concentration.***

*The ability to concentrate ensures success in any walk of life.*

Concentration means devoting total attention to a subject. If you want to learn well and get good marks in exams, then it is very important to avoid distractions. Just think of the subject which you want to concentrate on and banish all other things out of your mind. Sometimes, it goes beyond its limits and you tend to concentrate deeply on one subject while ignoring the others. This becomes an obsession at the cost of other subjects.

You must also learn to detach yourself from other things when you are concentrating on one particular subject. When you pick up the next subject, then you should detach yourself from the previous subject. This is the best way to concentrate on each subject. In simple words, to concentrate means to give your entire attention to a particular subject for a certain period and then to withdraw from it. After withdrawal, relax for a while and then move on to the other subject.

Make it a point not to study continuously for more than an hour. Take a break for a few minutes by getting up from your desk. You will come back refreshed and energised.

*Taking short breaks in between study hours improves concentration.*

Fortunately, the ability to concentrate can be learnt and developed. It begins with the **breathing process**.

- Sit comfortably in a chair.
- Concentrate on your breathing.
- Inhale deeply and count to ten.
- Hold the breath for some time.
- Release it slowly and repeat the process.

As your breathing becomes deeper, you will feel a burst of energy from within. Once you have mastered this process, you will find it very easy to concentrate on your studies.

## Let's grill you

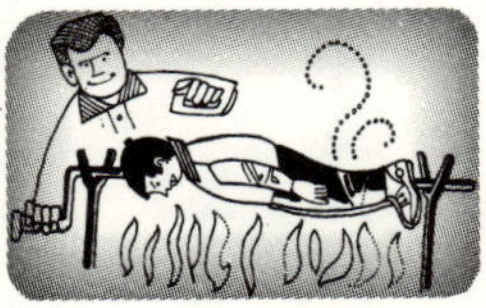

**Choose the correct answer to find out your level of concentration**

### *Marking key*

Give (1) mark to each 'a' answer and (2) marks to each 'b' answer.

**Marks**

1. After studying a subject for an hour, when you get up you feel— a/b ☐
   a. you need a break to relax.
   b. like shouting at everyone.
2. Whenever you try to concentrate on your book you— a/b ☐
   a. do so without much effort.
   b. keep on thinking about the interesting serial on television.

3. There is a marriage in the neighbourhood. The loudspeaker is blaring at full volume. You have to study for your exam which is on the following day. You— a/b ☐
   a. try to minimise the sound by drawing the curtains and get on with studies.
   b. you close the book and go to sleep.
4. When you get good marks in your test, you know— a/b ☐
   a. that it was your hard work.
   b. it was out of sheer luck.
5. You feel that concentration— a/b ☐
   a. ensures success.
   b. is an illusion.

☐

### Interpretation

- The lesser are your marks, the greater is your concentration. So improve your concentration by doing breathing exercise if you have scored higher points in the above drill. Remember, achievements in every field have been possible because of concentration on particular subjects. Even though the capacity to concentrate varies from one individual to an other, you can learn and develop this ability in order to ensure success in life.

### Just Chill

*Raja Yoga* or Soul Consciousness is a simple yet effective technique to clear the mind and improve concentration. Visualise a star in the centre of your forehead and repeatedly affirm "I am happy, I am peaceful, I love everyone."

## 3 Sutra

# Adopt a Study Schedule

***Our education system has adopted a multidimensional approach. Today, many subjects are taught in school. Unfortunately, nobody teaches the students how to study them effectively. If this single aspect is properly understood, the overall performance of the students will improve. In today's competitive world, it is not so important to work hard. What is more important is to work smart. For effective learning, we should know how to achieve more in less time and with lesser effort. The best way to achieve this goal is by allotting a proper timetable for studies. When we adopt a timetable, we place a definite schedule of action before us. We mentally prepare ourselves to meet it. A timetable removes the uncertainty as to what we need to do or not to do. The timetable is the plan laid out before you and now it is up to you to implement it. Variations are a part of life. Like any other plan, the timetable should also be flexible enough to absorb these variations. A time cushion should be provided in the timetable.***

***The question arises, how do we plan a study schedule? A study schedule should be designed in such a manner that it leaves some time in between for relaxation for the student. But this break should not be utilised for activities like playing on the computer or watching TV. These activities distract you and make it difficult to return to study. A separate time must be allocated to these activities. The break should be used solely for relaxation. The basic purpose of the break should be to give the eyes and muscles some rest.***

***While preparing the study schedule, if you feel you will not be able to cover all the subjects everyday, then you can alternately study them while giving half an hour between the studies for revising all that you studied the previous day.***

In the end, remember that no two individuals respond in the same way. You must design your study schedule keeping your personal preferences in mind. More important than the schedule is the resolution to follow it religiously. Only then you can derive maximum benefit from it.

# Getting started

***Board exams were round the corner. Adi knew he had a lot of study material to cover in one month. Still he kept postponing his studies. Every day, new excuses kept cropping up. One day, it was the cricket match which could not be missed. Next day was his friend's birthday, so the whole day went into an outing. The third day he was too exhausted to even open the books and so on. A whole week passed by but he kept evading his studies. The result—lesser time left to study. Finally, the day of examination arrived and he was in a state of frenzy.***

*Achievers are self starters.*

The human mind enjoys great affinity for the known and explored vistas. To seek change is a very difficult step. To start something different from what we are already doing requires a lot of energy. Most of us fail to generate that motive power and thereby fail at the first step itself. There is always an initial resistance which makes us want to give up. Negative thoughts keep our mind occupied. we tell ourselves this is not going to work. We find a hundred reasons for not starting, just like our dear friend Adi. But remember, people who do this get stuck in their grooves.

So get started with your preparations as early as possible and do not wait for the peak examination time to arrive. No need to go into panic attack. Realise that your first test starts just now and not afterwards. If you manage to get started in time, then you have passed the first test successfully. No one can stop you from excelling in exams.

*Be in harmony with your inner self. Motivate yourself.*

**Early bird gets the worm**

- Recognise the opportunity
- Leave all the doubts aside
- Have faith in your abilities

- Think of a date when you plan to actually start
- Start with confidence
- Also decide how long it will take for you to do each task
- Spring into action, and,
- Get going

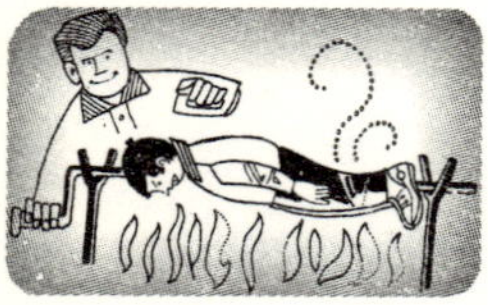

## Let's grill you

**Choose the correct answers and get started.**

### *Marking key*

Award (1) mark for each 'a' answer and (2) marks for each 'b' answer.

**Marks**

1. The day you decide to begin your studies, your friend invites you for a picnic. Would you— a/b ☐
   a. agree to go with him.
   b. tell him you will not be able to come.
2. If you keep postponing your study schedule, it— a/b ☐
   a. does not bother you at all.
   b. makes you feel guilty.
3. To get started, you are like a— a/b ☐
   a. handcart which needs to be pushed again and again.
   b. rocket which needs to be pushed once.
4. What motivates you to study— a/b ☐
   a. a good scolding from your mother.
   b. good grades.
5. You are considered an achiever in your group because— a/b ☐
   a. you have everything at home.
   b. you achieve your goals.

☐

### *Interpretation*

- **Below 6 :** If you have scored below 6, then you are not a self starter. You enjoy life as it comes and do not make an effort to excel in your pursuits. You need to boost up your spirits and take your studies seriously if you want to taste success in life.
- **Score 6 and above :** You understand the value of time. You manage to begin work on time so that you can finish it in the stipulated time. Do not be distracted by other things and concentrate on your goal to excel in life.

### *Just Chill*

Drink atleast one and a half litres of water every day.

It wakes you up, gives you more energy and gives your body the fluid it needs to function.

# Having a fixed timetable

***For his board exams, Ruchit started studying for four to five hours at a stretch. His parents took pride in his long study hours and praised him before everyone. Ruchit revelled in the praise and increased the number of hours he would study. When his results were declared, Ruchit was highly disappointed. He scored average marks in all the subjects despite putting in long hours of study everyday.***

***Where had Ruchit gone wrong?...***

*Study plans should be in harmony with personal preferences.*

It is an undisputed fact that you should have a definite timetable for study at home which should synchronise with your school timetable. It should include provisions for homework, revision and some time for making notes. But any work schedule must have provision for both study and leisure, as we all need to relax to boost our depleted energy levels at regular intervals.

Most parents lay undue emphasis on academics. But very long periods of study at a stretch are not good. Parents take pride that their child studies for three or four hours at a stretch. This is not the right approach. After a certain period of study, the mental receptivity of the child diminishes. Continuous study after this period does not benefit and no results accrue from such study.

*Action may not always bring happiness, but there is no happiness without action.*

Have you ever wondered why a period in school is never more than 45 minutes? This is because a person's receptivity for a subject is optimum for 40-45 minutes. Corresponding to this, the maximum period to study a subject at home should also be no more than one hour. Then a short break of ten minutes is helpful. Use your break to relax. Sitting in one posture builds physical tension in your body. A little movement relieves the muscles.

**Prepare a study schedule**

- Have separate timetables for school days and holidays.
- Allocate time equally for homework, revision and for making notes.
- Keep your timetable balanced with due importance to both study and leisure.
- Do not have long unbroken periods of study. It will hamper the learning process.
- For better receptivity, alternate various activities between study periods.
- Alternate different subjects for keeping a balanced interest in studies.

More significant than the schedule is the resolution to follow it religiously. Then only you can be sure of deriving maximum benefit from it.

## Let's grill you

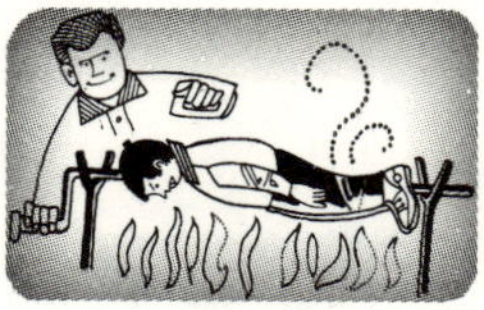

**We give below two timetables for a class X student. Which one do you think is correct? Tick in the box.**

***Timetable A***

| | |
|---|---|
| 8.00 a.m. – 2.00 p.m. | School |
| 2.00 p.m. – 3.00 p.m. | Lunch and relax |
| 3.00 p.m. – 5.00 p.m. | English |
| 5.00 p.m. – 6.00 p.m. | Hindi |
| 6.00 p.m. – 8.00 p.m. | Science |
| 8.00 p.m. – 9.00 p.m. | Social Studies |
| 9.00 p.m. – 9.20 p.m. | Dinner |
| 9.20 p.m. – 11.00 p.m. | Mathematics |
| 11.15 | Go to bed |

☐

### *Timetable B*

| | |
|---|---|
| 8.00 a.m. – 2.00 p.m. | School |
| 2.00 p.m. – 3.00 p.m. | Lunch and relax |
| 3.00 p.m. – 4.00 p.m. | Mathematics |
| 4.15 p.m. – 5.00 p.m. | English |
| 5.10 p.m. – 6.00 p.m. | Social Studies |
| 6.00 p.m. – 6.30 p.m. | A walk or outdoor activity |
| 6.30 p.m. – 7.15 p.m. | Hindi |
| 7.30 p.m. – 8.30 p.m. | Science |
| 8.30 p.m. – 9.15 p.m. | Dinner |
| 9.15 p.m.- 10.00 p.m. | Revision |
| 10.15 p.m. | Time to sleep |

☐

### *Interpretation*

- If you choose timetable A, then you may be trying to enter the studious category of students, but your approach is wrong. You have shown determination and will-power by choosing to spend the entire day studying, but you forgot that all work and no play makes Jack a dull boy. So give yourself short breaks between studies. Also choose different kinds of subjects to keep your interest alive. For example, by studying both English and Hindi one after the other, you will lose interest in them, as they are both Literature, and lengthy subjects which require reading skills. Space them by studying Mathematics or Science in between as they are analytical subjects and will divert your attention and counter boredom. Your day ends at 11.15 p.m., which is too late considering you have to wake up early to attend school at 8 o' clock.

- If you choose timetable B, then you are on the right track. The timetable has properly spaced subjects with required breaks between each subject. There is enough time for some outdoor activities and relaxation. The dinner break is also sufficient to let you eat in peace and relax for some time before you hit the books with renewed energy. Since you have to wake up early for school the next day, you must go to bed by 10.15 p.m., which is good enough to provide you sufficient sleep of eight hours so that you wake up refreshed to begin a new day.

### *Just Chill*

During your breaks, try something new and invigorating.

- Climb the stairs three times.
- Draw a cartoon of your favourite person.
- Squeeze some lemon and prepare a glass of lemonade for yourself.
- Stand in the balcony and watch the moving clouds in the sky.

# How to avoid distraction

***Aashima had three younger siblings—two brothers and a sister. The three of them would form a gang when they played and would create a ruckus. During her Board exams, Aashima found it difficult to concentrate on her studies with so much noise going on. Their mother tried to reason with them but they were too young to understand the gravity of the situation. They would keep quiet for a while but soon would forget all the instructions and start talking in loud voices. Though they played in a separate room, still it would distract Aashima so much that she was unable to concentrate. Aashima became so touchy that even their whispering would disturb her. Their mother was in a fix. She could not send the children out of the house nor could she send Aashima away to study. What was she to do?...***

If I tell you that for the next forty seconds do not think about food, what would happen? The first thing that comes to your mind is 'food'. That's the nature of the human mind. It gets swayed and distracted by any instruction that is out of the ordinary. In normal circumstances, your mind would not have thought about food at this moment, but now, since it has been specified, food occupies the foremost place in your thoughts. So learn to control your thoughts. They are your biggest source of distraction. A mind full of thoughts is like an ocean with high waves. Whatever you throw into it, no impact will be created. In contrast, a pebble thrown in a small pond will make ripples.

*If you want a rainbow, you have got to put up with the rain.*

There is no doubt that the most effective studies can be done in an environment where there is no distraction—from neighbours, from siblings, from television, from traffic, and so on. You name it and you have it. You have to use your own discretion as to how best you can handle each situation. In general, we give you a few places where you may study.

- Study in a library. The quiet and calm atmosphere is conducive to study. Just do not get distracted by other books there.
- Go to your friend's place for group study. Beware of distracting sessions of leisure talks on other topics.
- Go to the terrace to study. The chirping of birds, the blaring sirens and loudspeakers may distract you more there, and if you happen to be a nature lover, then you will certainly spend more time in admiring nature than your books.

*The greatest source of distraction is your own thoughts.*

The sky is the limit for your imagination, but try these four things before you let your imagination run wild–

**a. Avoid** – Avoid the distraction. Suppose you like to watch a certain serial on TV, then either do not sit to study at that time or study at a place where you cannot have access to the TV.

**b. Change** – Change the situation by taking action. Suppose a sibling is irritating you and you do not want to hurt him, then explain the situation to him or study when he is also occupied elsewhere.

**c. Eliminate** – The noise factor can also be eliminated easily by the use of earplugs. It is a worthwhile investment if you are constantly disturbed by the noise.

**d. Accept** – Finally, when nothing works, the best option is to simply accept the situation as it is. Suddenly, you will find that it is no longer distracting you. You have successfully controlled your thoughts.

# Let's grill you

In the first column, write down five major distractions for your study and mentally decide the strategy for each distraction. In the second column, write down the ways in which you plan to overcome these distractions.

| | ***Distractions*** | ***How to overcome these distractions*** |
|---|---|---|
| 1. | | |
| 2. | | |
| 3. | | |
| 4. | | |
| 5. | | |

After writing them down, you will find it much easier to deal with the source of distraction.

***Just Chill***

Let the light shine through and energy flow freely.

If the windows in your room are dirty, then your outlook on the world is clouded.

If your windows are clean and light gets through in abundance, then your view will be crystal clear.

# Self-discipline

***Preparing a timetable to study regularly is very important. But more important than that is to be able to stick to it. Simi had made such a time-table and she was trying very hard to follow it. But whenever something distracted her, she would leave her studies aside and get involved in other things. This distraction could be her favourite serial on TV or her friend's phone call or her brother calling her to play a game of chess. As it always happens in such cases, she missed one day of studies, then another day, and then began a typical cycle of missing studies every day. It was so easy to return to her old pattern but how difficult to stick to the new study schedule. It required self-discipline.***

*Self-discipline is the first step to success.*

Most of us perceive discipline as something which is imposed upon us against our will. In a way it is true because it is human nature to shake off everything that is forced upon them. But the truth remains that one cannot succeed without a certain discipline. Take, for instance, our universe, where planets move according to a predetermined system. Seasons change in a definite rhythm. Nature responds to them in the same way, year after year. If this discipline broke down, there would be total chaos. Life on earth would perish.

*I do not have the key to success but the key to failure is definitely to try and please everyone.*

In the same way, human success too depends upon discipline. Self-discipline begins with each of us understanding ourselves well. We are all a combination of good and bad qualities. We must be aware of our strengths and weaknesses. Then we can lay greater emphasis on our strengths and take steps to transform our weaknesses into strengths.

Charting your progress is another path leading to self-discipline. All you have to do is to decide your target in each subject. Prepare a study chart which can have lesson numbers, dates and your target for each date. Make a tick mark on each date and the number of lessons you completed on that date. If it meets your target, then tick on the target too.

Believe me, each tick on your target will boost your self-confidence and your level of self-discipline. The satisfaction that you will get out of putting that tick will be motivation enough for you to excel in exams.

## Let's grill you

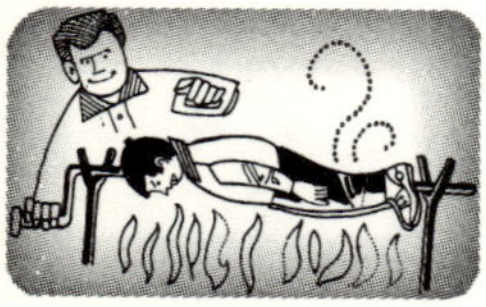

Chart your strengths and weaknesses in this table and also write how you intend to turn your weaknesses into strengths.

| | |
|---|---|
| **Strengths** | |
| **Weaknesses** | |
| **Ways to improve** | |

***Just Chill***

Sometimes it is hard to say 'No'. You have to decide whether you want to be a nice person or less stressed out and therefore, nicer!

Sutra 4

# Mastering Skills

*You are known by your abilities. These abilities depend upon your learning and skills. To develop skills, you need to reinforce strengths and steadily overcome weaknesses. For this, you need to have brainpower. Just like your body, your mind also has power. How far you can stretch your brain-power depends upon how strong it is. Your ability to develop skills largely depends upon your brainpower. You must have met people with extraordinary skills. These skills have been achieved after labour of many years. So the first step towards mastering skills is making your mind extra strong. Solving puzzles and crosswords as well as creative visualisation are some of the best brain teasers which make use of different faculties of the brain. Logic and lateral thinking puzzles are specially recommended for improving brainpower.*

*One of the best exercises is speed counting. Count the numbers in simple sequence upto 100 and then back to 1. Now give gaps of 1 and count from 1 to 99 and back to 1. Slowly increase the gaps. Give gaps of 2—starting from 2 to 98 and back to 2. Similarly with gaps of 3—from 3 to 99*

***and back to 3. You can keep increasing the gaps upto 9. This exercise is really mind-blowing, if you are able to do this exercise at a good speed. While doing this, you will actually feel the pressure on your brain.***

***There are other similar exercises like reverse alphabets from Z to A, alternate alphabets like a,c,e,....and their reverse z,x,v ......... You may even try to double a number as long as you can. You may even learn poems, songs and try to sing them backwards.***

***Basically, you can do anything that challenges your mind. Most of the time our brain is busy thinking. Needless to say, thinking improves problem solving abilities and grasping power. But there is a catch! Useless thoughts that entertain your brain are useless. They do nothing to your brain in terms of boosting its power.***

So to develop skills, you need to reinforce strengths and steadily overcome weaknesses. This is a gradual process which can be achieved if you have a strong mind and great will-power. Get down to it and success will follow you soon.

# Having good observation

***When Ria went to Goa, she enjoyed herself thoroughly. She tried a new Goan dish, and was impressed by the beauty scattered all around the beaches. When she came back, she described in detail the delicious dish she had eaten in Goa, but when her friends asked her about her drive to the countryside, the beaches and the malls, she could remember things only fleetingly. Was her observation really so bad?***

*People with good observation are good learners.*

To have good observation is to be able to notice important details. When we employ all the senses, the observation power increases. The more the senses used in observing a particular situation, the better our memory will be about it. That is the reason why Ria remembered details of food, as all the senses including sight, smell, taste and touch are used. The crackling sound of a crisp dish, heard while eating it, completes the observation. In comparison, only a few things are remembered which involve only sight.

Similarly, in the process of learning and gaining knowledge, observation plays a very significant part. In a lecture, we remember what we see or hear. Reading reinforces our memory of what we have learnt. In practical classes or excursions, we use our sight, hearing and sense of touch also. It makes our observation powers better. Good observation is the key to a good memory.

Remember, people with a good memory have keen observation. They are quick to analyse things and associate them with existing knowledge. If they cannot comprehend information immediately, then they take notes and revise them later. You very well know by now that information gradually fades away with disuse. This makes it necessary that whatever information is important must be reinforced periodically through revision.

*You may complain because roses have thorns or you may rejoice because thorns have roses.*

# Let's grill you

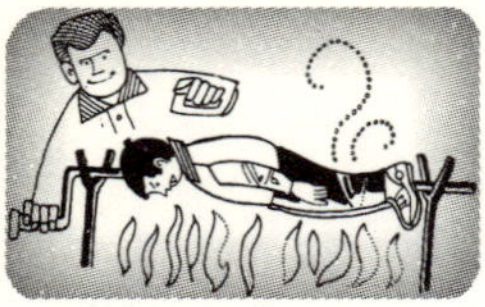

**Do some of these exercises and check your observation power.**

1. Open your fridge, note any ten things in it and close the door. Write down the names of all these ten items on a piece of paper and check your list.
   - **If you have written half or more names of things correctly, then you have a good observation power.**
2. Make a list of all the students in your class. Write one good quality in each of them. Did you get it right?
   - **If yes, then your observation power is good.**
3. Open a book and read a lesson carefully. After you finish reading, close your eyes and try to visualise the page in your mind.
   - **If the page comes to you clearly, you have a good observation power.**
4. When you study, do you just go on reading or you make notes alongside.
   - **If you do, then your observation powers are good.**
5. Do you associate things with your known things to gain knowledge quickly.
   - **If you do, then you enjoy a good observation power.**

Having a good observation power is a virtue. If you are a good observer, then you are a keen learner. Analyse carefully what you observe and note it down on paper, because if you use as many senses as possible while making observations, then you can easily excel in exams.

# In the wonderland of exams

***When the new syllabus of the CBSE was introduced some years ago, there was apprehension among the teachers as to how students would adapt to the new system. The old system was simple and easy. The teacher would teach the chapter, (in most cases, a reading would suffice), dictate the answers and the test was given from those questions alone. There was not much effort required on the part of the students. All they needed to do was to cram the portions marked by the teacher. The new system was divided into learning skills, writing skills, project work, preparing seminars, extempore, making models, charts and understanding the lessons in totality. The simple process of cramming had turned into a full-time job of churning out all-rounder students. The initial resistance, however, gave way to enthusiastic cheers when the results were found to be encouraging. The students gained much more with this form of study. Today almost all the schools have adopted this system.***

*Every exam aims at testing students differently.*

What is Alice doing in the wonderland of exams? Trying to figure out what comes next!

Exams test our skills. They begin at the lowest level when small children are tested for their repetitive skills and handwriting. As they grow up, the tests become harder with students learning to deal with multiple choice questions where they have to choose objectively between two or three options.

*You will get what you deserve. What is meant for you, no one can take away from you; what is not meant for you, no power on earth will allow you to keep it.*

As time passes, tests become exams and you require both an understanding of the subject and the ability to put the knowledge across in writing. There are monthly tests and quarterly, half-yearly and final exams at the school level. At each exam, there may be a fixed number of questions to be answered.

Later in life, during competitive exams, both objective as well as subjective type questions are asked, to judge your abilities. By now it is evident that one method is not right to tackle every exam. The methods of learning remain the same but the pattern of each exam varies. So you need to use all your skills as you adapt according to need each time.

## Let's grill you

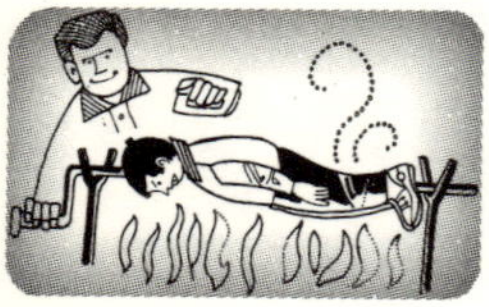

**Let's see how you rate exams in your life. Answer these questions carefully.**

### *Marking key*

For each 'Yes' give yourself (1) mark and for each 'No', do not give any mark.

| | | | Marks |
|---|---|---|---|
| 1. | It is important to know what to expect in exams. | Yes/No | ☐ |
| 2. | We should not hate exams as they are a part of our growing up years. | Yes/No | ☐ |
| 3. | Students who study regularly always do well. | Yes/No | ☐ |
| 4. | We should relax before the exams and avoid tensions. | Yes/No | ☐ |
| 5. | Exams aim at all-round development of our personality. | Yes/No | ☐ |
| | | | ☐ |

### *Interpretation*

- **Scores 3–5 :** You have understood the importance of exams in your life. You are comfortable with exams now and you make efforts to get good marks through studying.
- **Scores 0–2 :** However much you may like to deny, the truth remains that you cannot avoid exams. So why not accept this fact now, when there is still time to improve.

### *Just Chill*

If you have a headache, apply pressure to the top of your big toe—reflexology links the toe with the head.

# Doing selective study

***Just before her Board exams, Neha came down with chicken pox. She did not have much time left to study for her first paper which was Physics. Neha was very tense. It was at this moment that her teacher told her about selective study. She told Neha to revise the chapters she already knew well, till she learnt them by heart. She told her to skip the unstudied portion. In this way, she was sure of scoring in the topics she had learnt carefully. There was no point in being Jack of all trades and master of none. Teacher also told Neha to read the unstudied portion later, if she had time. And even among that portion, she told Neha to pick up the part which appeared to be the most interesting to her.***

*Selective study is all about doing less things in more details than doing more things with less details.*

After years of empirical study, Sir Pareto gave us the principle of 20:80. He made a powerful observation based on this principle—

**20% causes are responsible for 80% effects**.

It implies that there is a critical part of every object, process and action. This critical part affects a major part of the results.

But one thing should be remembered clearly that selective study should be used in case of emergency only. Normally, an average student who studies regularly throughout the year need not resort to this method of selective study. However, there are always chances of an emergency in everyone's life. So it would be fitting to empower yourself with this powerful method.

*The first step towards solving a problem is to begin.*

### Preconditions attached to selective study

- Selective study must only be used when the need arises.
- It is not a luxury to which you should not resort to, often.

- Before you choose to do selective study, make sure your question paper will have a lot of options.

**How to do selective study**

- Find out the weightage of each chapter in your syllabus.
- Select the chapters which you have read before, for selective study.
- Focus on what you already know, till you know it perfectly.
- Do not even think of the unstudied portion.
- Ensure that the marks that you score in questions asked from the portion you have studied in selective study will be maximum.
- If you have time after perfecting the chapters you have selected for selective study – go to the unread part.
- Pick up the portion that appears most interesting to you.
- Do it in true detail.

In short, while doing selective study, you have to be true to yourself and use it only in case of emergencies.

## Let's grill you

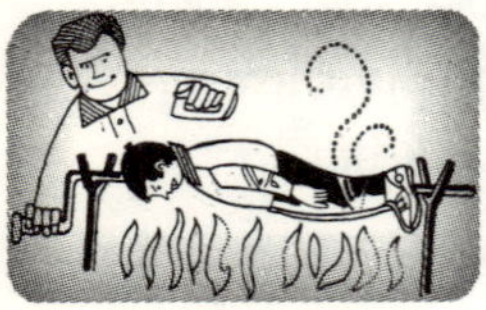

**Tick the statements which you feel are acceptable for selective study. Give reasons for your answer.**

1. Ramesh is down with viral fever. His exams are fast approaching. He feels he should do selective study.

Answer:

2. Rajesh's father died in an accident. He went into a shock. It took him almost three months to come out of it. His exams are fast approaching. Only 15 days are left. Do you think he should resort to selective study?

Answer:

3. Ridhima came to Delhi from Kolkata when her father got transferred here. Her school in Kolkata followed the State Board pattern. Here, she got admission to a school which followed the CBSE pattern. Some of the chapters were the similar but some were entirely new to her. Her exams were fast approaching. She decided to resort to selective study.

Answer:

4. Ruchi had a ball throughout the year. She hardly ever sat down to study. Now, as the exams are fast approaching, she is having butterflies in her stomach. She feels the best way out is to do selective study.

Answer:

### *Interpretation*

- Rajesh and Ridhima have a genuine reason to do selective study. They are facing problems in life which cause for corrective measures. Ramesh and Ruchi, however, should take their studies seriously and not resort to the selective study method.

### *Just Chill*

When in doubt, remember these lines, "God grant me the serenity to accept the things I cannot change, the courage to change the things I can, and the wisdom to know the difference."

# Bluff your way in

***Suhail was an average student. He always got good marks in exams even though he was never considered to be a studious child. Robin, on the other hand, always had his nose buried in books. Still, when the results were declared, his score would be less than Suhail's score. One day Robin checked Suhail's answer sheet and he found that though there was not much depth in the matter, Suhail's way of presenting the answers was superior than his own. While Robin used to write all the relevant matter in a paragraph, Suhail had covered only half of that matter but wrote it in points and illustrated them with appropriate diagrams. In his next exam, Robin tried the same technique and managed to score good marks. He was very happy. He had hit upon the magic formula of intelligent bluffing.***

*Blessed is the student who knows the delicate art of intelligent bluffing.*

What Suhail is doing is called intelligent bluffing. Many times we are faced with a situation where we are not sure of the facts. It may be a question that we have never heard before or something that we learnt but forgot. Most students will leave such a question, scared of it and at a loss for words. But wemay save the situation by intelligent bluffing.

*Don't fret about what others are thinking about you. They are busy fretting over what you are thinking about them.*

**Psychology of the examiner**

Before you attempt intelligent bluffing for a question, make sure you have answered everything that you know well first. If you bluff in the first question itself, be ready to be exposed. By the time your examiner approaches the bluffed question, he has already corrected some fabulous answers written by you. He should be really impressed by your presentation by now. He is in a very positive frame of mind about your paper now. His attention span, which was at its peak at the start of the paper is now slowly diminishing. He is under the assumption that you are a good student.

**How to bluff it**

- A bluffed answer has two important parts. They are at the start and at the end. The attention of the examiner is highest at these points. You must appreciate that it is also easy to bluff in these parts, thereby convincing the examiner that you have written the best answer.
- Start with a vague description about the answer. Keep it very general so that no mistakes are ever detected.

- Try to recollect all that you know about the topic and use the keywords in the beginning.
- In this way, you may fool the examiner in believing that you know the concepts.
- Use the middle part of the answer mainly for expanding on the things that you could recollect.
- End your answer with a convincing conclusion.

## Let's grill you

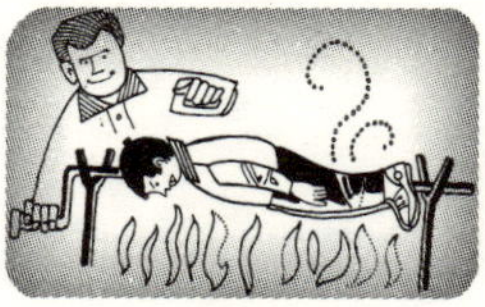

**Given below are the two paragraphs on Mahatma Gandhi. You have to judge which one shows intelligent bluffing.**

(1) Gandhiji was born on 2nd October, 1869 at Porbandar in Gujarat. After completing his initial education in India, he went to England to study law. After he became a lawyer, he went to South Africa where he had his first brush with British apathy towards racism. He came back and decided to fight the British through non-violence. He died on 30th January, 1948.

• ........................

(2) Gandhiji's birth was the most significant event of the nineteenth century. He was born on 2nd October. He was a Gujarati. After completing his initial education, he wanted to pursue law. He became a lawyer. But seeing the poor condition of Indians, he decided to become a freedom fighter and free India from British rule. He advocated non-violence. Soon after India got independence, Gandhiji was killed, and our country lost a great leader.

- ...............................

### *Interpretation*

- (2) is the paragraph which demonstrates intelligent bluffing. The student does not remember all the facts, specially the dates associated with the events. But he has a general idea of the situation. So he manages a good show by intelligent bluffing.

### *Just Chill*

Learn from the kids to smile from one eye and to shed tears from the other eye. Children forget their insults and hurts very quickly, and do not boast about their achievements either.

# Making good notes

***Raji was struggling with her Biology lessons when her friend Vasudha came to her house. She asked Raji to show her the notes so that she could clear a few points. Raji showed her ignorance. Vasudha got very angry thinking Raji did not want to share her notes with her. She left immediately. But this set Raji thinking. She was not lying. She had never made any notes in her life, so how could she share them with Vasudha? Now, the point to ponder on was how to make notes?.......***

Making notes is the most important skill towards greater success in exams. Everyone makes notes but not everyone knows how to make good notes. It is not enough to make notes. They must also be clear and understandable. They should be written in such a way that a glance should enable you to recall the entire subject. Good notes must be simple, well organised and easy to understand.

At school, many teachers dictate notes that you could rely upon. But these notes are available for the entire class. So they put you at par with the other students. If you wish to excel, instead of depending entirely upon these notes, you should make your own notes. On returning home from school, the ideal situation will be to revise what has been taught from the textbook and create notes incorporating the matter given by the teacher. In this way, the revision helps better understanding of the subject and puts it in the long term memory.

*Good notes enable fast revision before exams.*

### Making notes effectively

- Select the matter for which you want to make notes.
- Condense it and organise it logically.

- Simplify the language and use your own words while making notes. This will also improve your writing skills.
- Good notes must be simple, well-organised and easy to understand.
- Use figures and diagrams wherever required.

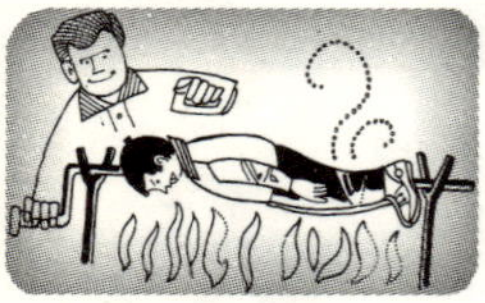

## Let's grill you

**Mark your choice in the following statements.**

***Marking key***

Give (2) marks for each 'a' answer and (1) mark for each 'b' answer.

**Marks**

1. When I reach home after a tedious day at school, I prefer to— a/b ☐
   a. take it easy till the next day.
   b. relax for a while and then sit down to revise what was taught in school.
2. I use the notes given by the teacher for— a/b ☐
   a. revision in exams.
   b. preparing my own notes.
3. My notes are made in such a way that when I open them during exams— a/b ☐
   a. I have to refer to the book instead.
   b. they are sufficient for me to revise.
4. Sharing my notes with others— a/b ☐
   a. I don't mind.
   b. No way. They are the fruit of my own labour.
5. After preparing my own notes, I keep them— a/b ☐
   a. anywhere.
   b. in a secure place where I can find them easily during exams.

☐

### *Interpretation*

- **Scores 7-10 :** You may be good at studies but your attitude towards making notes is simply too easygoing. It will take you some time before you realise the importance of notes. You do not believe in the saying *Neither a lender, nor a borrower be,* because you do not value your notes. Try to make proper notes this time and see the difference in your performance.
- **Scores 1-6 :** It is good that you understand the value of notes in studies. You have the right attitude towards them and your studies. Keep it up and nothing can stop you from scoring good marks in exams.

### *Just Chill*

Do something that uses a part of the brain that you don't normally use—like doing Maths without a calculator.

It stimulates your brain and you feel inspired.

5

Sutra

# Memory Boosters

***Before we talk about boosting our memory, we must understand what exactly is memory. For easy understanding, we may compare memory to a filing cabinet in which different documents are stored for later use. How well or how systematically we store these documents will only be tested when we are asked to retrieve them at a later date. If we are able to retrieve them immediately, then our filing system is considered good, otherwise it is not up to the mark. This is exactly what happens with our memory. If we are able to retrieve the information and put it on paper during exams within the allocated time, then we score well. If the information cannot be retrieved in time, then it is obviously of no use.***

To get the best out of our memory system, we must understand how the memory process works. It works in five steps—

### 1. Attention

A lot of primary information is generated through our sense of seeing, hearing and doing—as visual memory, auditory memory and kinaesthetic memory respectively. Generally, memory constitutes 65%

visual, 20% auditory and 15% kinaesthetic perceptions.

## 2. Selection

Everything that we see, hear, smell or touch generates information. Innumerable messages are being received all the time. So it becomes necessary to select messages that we wish to store.

*Each man is the architect of his own fate.*

## 3. Encoding

The third step is to encode the selected message on the basis of acoustic code, (sound) visual code (look) or semantic code (meaning). The way you encode information affects its recall.

## 4. Storage

Memory can be short term memory (STM) or long term memory (LTM). STM is brief and transient, like a telephone number that you may remember till you dial it. As the name suggests, it holds a small amount of information for a limited period. LTM stays with you for a long time and can be retrieved at a later date, like driving a car or riding a bicycle or any other skill. If STM has to be converted into long term memory, it is transferred through repetition or through association with a past memory or via regular use of information. That is why we remember the telephone numbers which we use frequently, or we remember those chapters which we study daily even for a short period.

## 5. Memory recall

Retrieval of memory is just the opposite of encoding. Retrieval becomes easy if we follow a definite system for encoding. Suppose we use an acoustic code for encoding, we can retrieve the information by using the same code for retrieval. The best example for this can be a lullaby which is encoded in our subconscious and comes back to us when we hear it or sing it.

# Improving memory

***Savita crammed for her exam day and night. But when she sat down to give her exam, she felt everything fly out of her mind. She failed to recall even half the things she had learnt so well. She felt like crying....***

Haven't we all faced the same predicament at some point of time in life? We call it bad memory. But the truth is that there is nothing such as a good memory or a bad memory. The difference between our retention power is due to a trained and an untrained memory. People with good memory are not specially blessed in any way. Their better memory is because of better observation power, evaluation and training. Memory is like any other body function. Use it regularly and you can depend upon it. But when you do not use it, it fades and becomes worthless.

*A good memory can make a sophisticated computer look crude.*

You cannot improve memory by taking certain medicines. This thought lures many youngsters. But all these are wrong notions. If such was the case, wouldn't we all become masters in the memory game.

It is true that lack of certain nutrients in the food does affect one's receptivity of knowledge. Providing a balanced meal is the simplest solution for this problem.

So the best way to improve memory is **Memory Training**. You must understand the working of the memory. Memory works through association. When you come across some unknown information, you will search for something known or common. As soon as you will find that, you will make a link. This process of linking one thing to another is called understanding. **Visualisation** also helps in understanding and in turn helps in improving memory.

*Memory depends mainly on the association of thoughts and ideas.*

Remember, the more the information present in your brain, the better the chances of finding neuro-associations. So, instead of saving your memory to decay, it's time to start using it. Believe me, it will help.

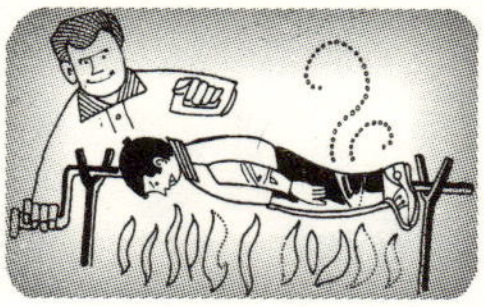

## Let's grill you

1. Read the five words given below and recollect them in similar order.

   - **car, carrot, Sania Mirza, dandia, eggs**

   Now, if you look at them once and try to remember them, then you are most likely to forget the order in the next instant. So you have to visualise them in a story, forming various links.

**The story**

Visualise a car full of carrots going on the road. Car is linked to the carrots.

The second link may be Sania playing tennis with dandia sticks instead of a racket and using eggs in place of balls.

Given below are two such sets. Make your own stories and links.

A. **coffee, kingfisher, pond, cloud, cow**

B. **Saurav Ganguly, computer, telephone, bulb, toffee**

2. Play this memory game with your friends. Sit in a circle. Moving clockwise, the first one may say, 'I like to eat potatoes.' The next one will say, 'I like to eat potatoes and tomatoes.' The next one will add one more vegetable in the same sentence. In this way, each person adds a new vegetable to the list. The person who cannot repeat the list correctly is eliminated. The last person to repeat the list correctly is

the winner. This game improves hearing, receptivity and memory. You may even have variations in the game by using different things or rephrasing the sentence.

In the next few pages, we give you a few memory enhancing techniques which shall help you train your mind.

***Just Chill***

Put this book down and take a walk for 5 minutes. Look around to see what life is doing right now. It is really easy to focus on yourself and what you are doing all the time.

So remember to look around and go for a refreshing stroll to clear your mind.

# Novelex

Novelex means **Novel Exercises**. Novelex is based on the fact that the human brain hungers for novelty. It is designed to respond to new information coming from the outside world. The brain gets stimulated when novel and unexpected stimuli are presented.

Novelex uses the senses in novel ways to break out of everyday routine. The non routine and unexpected experiences are used with various combinations of our physical senses—vision, hearing, taste, smell and touch. These five senses help in developing the brain's natural drive to form associations between different types of information.

*To know and not to do, is not yet 'to know.'*

## Novelex techniques

- Involve a new sense for doing the routine task. For example, get dressed for school with your eyes closed or comb your hair with your eyes closed. Your hands will notice various textures of your own hair which you may not be aware of earlier.
- Use your non-dominant hand. If you are right handed, start using your left hand for daily jobs like brushing your teeth, buttoning shirts, handling food, turning off the switches etc. When you use your left hand, then your right brain is stimulated, which you rarely stimulate.
- Use different gadgets. If you are used to writing with a pen, use a pencil or an ink pen this time.
- Try different routes on way to school. When you go on your normal route, your brain goes into automatic mode and is not at all stimulated. A new route arouses all your senses and they become alert.

*Treat everybody with politeness, even those who are rude to you. Remember that you show courtesy to others not because they are gentlemen but because you are one.*

- Reading aloud stimulates your brain. If you want to read fast, silent reading is recommended. Silent reading activates only one area of the cortex in the left hemisphere but listening to words activates three distinct brain areas.
- Try different cuisine occasionally. Try to identify the food items in your plate only through the sense of smell. You may also change the order of eating. For example, start with dessert and end with soup. Try it, your brain will thank you for such a change.
- Plan a vacation. Visit new places and interact with new people. The more you travel, the more will be your brainpower because travel broadens your vision and perception and stimulates the brain.
- Write something creative.
- Learn a new language. You may also try to learn sign language. Better still, create your own sign language in association with your friends.
- Constantly change the pattern of whatever you are doing. Once in a while, reposition the furniture or study table in your room. Your brain will be stimulated to adjust to the new surroundings.

***Just Chill***

Give your mother an evening off and you cook a simple meal for the family. The family will welcome the change in flavour, and you will enjoy the change in routine.

# Mind mapping

Mind mapping uses visual images and other graphic details to make a deeper impression. Mind mapping is based on the fact that the brain often recalls information easily in the form of pictures, symbols, sounds, shapes and feelings. It is easier than traditional methods of note taking because it activates both sides of the brain. It is also relaxing, fun and creative.

Mind mapping helps you to prepare notes from the textbooks. It is a 'whole brain approach' through which an entire subject can be displayed on one page. It is easier to remember the details from a mind map because it is written in a form that your brain naturally follows.

### How to make a mind map

- Start with taking a paper and coloured pens.
- You may turn the paper sideways to provide more space.
- Write the main topic in the middle and enclose it within a circle, square or any other shape you fancy.
- Add a branch extending out from the centre for each important point. The number of branches will vary with the number of segments. You may use different colours for each branch or segment.
- Write a keyword on each branch.
- Build it out to add details.
- These keywords should be such that they trigger your memory when you look at them.
- You can also use abbreviations, but be sure to be familiar with them so you will instantly be able to identify what they stand for, even at a later date.

*Be happy with what you have, while working for what you want.*

- You may add symbols and illustrations for better recall.
- Make important ideas larger so they will jump out at you when you read your notes.
- Underline words. Use bold letters wherever required.
- Most importantly, whatever you write should be legible and clear.

Initially, mind mapping will require some effort, creativity and imagination on your part, but soon you will get used to it and it will be an easy task for you. The brain is extraordinarily stimulated in mind mapping and it also helps you to recall the topics at a later date.

*Each one of us cannot do great things but we can do small things greatly.*

***Just Chill***

Let me share a very interesting story with you. It is about Everybody, Somebody, Anybody and Nobody. These are the names of the four heroes of our story. Once, there was an important job to be done. Everybody was sure Somebody would do it. Anybody could have done it but Nobody did it. Somebody got angry because it was Everybody's job. Everybody thought Anybody could do it but Nobody realised that Everybody wouldn't do it. It ended up that Everybody blamed Somebody when Nobody did what Anybody could have done!

The reason why most jobs remain piled up!

# Magic squares

A magic square is an intriguing device where a big square is divided into a number of smaller squares. A set of different numbers is arranged in a particular pattern to form a grid in such a way that the sum of the numbers in each row, each column and diagonals adds up to the same number. Magic squares boost your brainpower and they are a great pastime too.

*Problems come to us to make us think.*

***The story of magic square goes way back many centuries before the birth of Christ when a tortoise crawled out of the Yellow River in China. On its back was present a strange pattern of dots. When these dots were converted into numbers, the sum of the numbers vertically, horizontally and diagonally was found to be the same. People were amazed at it. They tried to construct similar patterns with different sets of numbers and also with varied patterns of squares. This is how the magic square was born.***

*Never think that your problems are forever. They will pass away like a cloud.*

Given below are two magic squares which you may fill in and improve your brainpower.

**A nine-cell magic square**

| | | |
|---|---|---|
| 8 | 1 | |
| 3 | | 7 |
| 4 | 9 | |

Total .......

**Ans.**

| | | |
|---|---|---|
| 8 | 1 | 6 |
| 3 | 5 | 7 |
| 4 | 9 | 2 |

Total - 15

### A twenty-five-cell magic square

| 23 | 6 | 19 | 2 | 15 |
|---|---|---|---|---|
| 10 | 18 |  | 14 |  |
| 17 | 5 | 13 | 21 |  |
| 4 |  | 25 | 8 | 16 |
|  | 24 | 7 | 20 |  |

Total ......

**Ans.**

| 23 | 6 | 19 | 2 | 15 |
|---|---|---|---|---|
| 10 | 18 | 1 | 14 | 22 |
| 17 | 5 | 13 | 21 | 9 |
| 4 | 12 | 25 | 8 | 16 |
| 11 | 24 | 7 | 20 | 3 |

Total - 65

### Tips on how to construct a square

You can even construct your own magic squares by following the given pattern.

Nine-cell magic square (3X3)

a) • Start with number 1 just above the centre cell of the box

• No. 2 should be placed on the corner box at bottom right

• Numbers 3, 4, 5, 6, 7, 8, 9 should be arranged as shown in the above magic square

• If you follow this pattern, then by multiplying the middle number (5 for the above square) with 3 (number of cells in each row) you will get the total for all sides. (5×3=15)

b) • Keep adding 2 to each number of the magic square. Their sequence remains the same.

• 5+2=7

So, in the bottom right corner put 4(2+2). Similerly put 9(7+2) above 4, and put 8(6+2) in the top right corner, This gives us a total of 21.

# Brainex

Brainex involves mental exercises. These exercises change the chemistry and structure of our synapses. Solving puzzles, riddles, mathematical and accounting problems can be considered good mental exercises. Since my purpose is not to test your mathematical or accounting skills, we shall ask you only puzzles and riddles which will refresh you and provide some exercise to the brain. Don't worry about the answers. They are given at the end of the chapter.

*If you can dream it, you can do it.*

1. **Elizabeth's mother had four children. The first child was named June, the second July, and the third August. What is the name of the fourth child?**
2. **Divide 50 by half and add 20. From the sum, subtract 35. What do you get?**
3. **The ages of a father and son add up to 55. The father's age is the son's age reversed. How old are they?**
4. **Often talked about, never seen, ever coming, never been, daily looked for, never here, still approaching, coming near. We all wait for its visit, but alas for our fate, we never find it here. What is it?**
5. **A bottle and a cork together cost Rs. 150 and the bottle costs Rs. 100 more than the cork. How much does each cost?**
6. **Write the next number in the series 4,9,25,49,(?)**
7. **Four cars came to a crossroads at the same time, each coming from a different direction. All the drivers were in a hurry and proceeded fast without stopping at the crossroads. They did not crash into each other. How is it possible?**

8. If 9th April falls two days after tomorrow i.e. Wednesday, then what would be the last day of the month?

9. A's watch is running 10 minutes slow but he is under the impression that it is only 5 minutes slow. B's watch is running 10 minutes fast, but he is under the impression that it is only 5 minutes fast. Both A and B reach a particular place at 4 o'clock according to their calculations. At what time would they reach there if their watches showed the correct time?

10. How is your father's only brother's wife's only brother-in-law related to you?

11. I cultivate carrots in my kitchen garden. One day I took some carrots to the market. I sold half for tomatoes and ate 4 carrots myself. Then I sold half of the remaining carrots for apples and ate 3 carrots. Afterwards I ate one (1) carrot and sold half for bananas. This left me with 5 carrots. How many carrots did I take to the market to sell?

12. X and Y are two brothers. B is A's brother but A is the mother of X. What is B to Y?

13. How can 4 be half of 5?

14. How can you make the equation true by drawing only one straight line:

    5+5+5 = 550

15. A bus leaves from the Delhi bus stand every 30 minutes. An enquiry clerk told a passenger that the bus had already left ten minutes earlier and the next bus would leave at 9.35 a.m. At what time did the enquiry clerk give this information to the passenger?

**16.** **How would you rearrange the letters in the words 'new door' to make one word?**

**17.** **Two babies were born on the same day, same year, with the same mother and father but are not twins. How is it possible?**

**18.** **A murderer is condemned to death. He has to choose between three rooms. He is told the first is full of raging fires, the second is full of mad assassins with loaded guns and the third is full of huge lions who have not eaten for six months. Which room should he choose?**

**19.** **Six glasses are in a row. The first three are filled with milk and the last three are empty. By moving only one glass, can you rearrange them so that the full and empty glasses alternate.**

**20.** **A is younger than C but older than B. D is younger than B. C is older than A, but younger than E. Who is the youngest and who is the oldest?**

## Answers

1. Elizabeth (as she is the fourth child).
2. 85. When you divide 50 by half you will get 100 and not 25 as you must have thought.
3. The father is 41 and the son is 14.
4. Tomorrow.
5. The bottle costs Rs. 125 and the cork costs Rs. 25.
6. 121. All the numbers in the row are the squares of prime numbers, therefore, it is 11 squared = 121.
7. They all turned to the left side.
8. It will also be a Wednesday.

9. A's watch = 4.05 and B's watch = 3.55.
10. He is your father.
11. 64 carrots (64/2 = 32-4 = 28/2 = 14-3 = 11-1 = 10/2 = 5
12. Uncle
13. The Roman numeral IV appears in the middle of the English word FIVE – F(IV)E.
14. 545 + 5 = 550
15. 9.15 a.m.
16. 'One word'
17. They are triplets
18. He should choose the third room because lions that have not eaten for six months would obviously be dead!
19. Pick up the second glass and pour half the milk into the fifth glass and then put it back in the second position.
20. ECABD. D is the youngest and E is the oldest.

***Just Chill***

Whine less, breathe more
Talk less, say more
Hate less, love more
And all good things will be yours.

6

Sutra

# Study Techniques

Temptations are all around us. They seem to be increasing every day with new discoveries and inventions. The TV, computer, and mobile phone are the top three distractions. So before you adopt those study techniques which help you to study effectively, you need to learn to control your urge to be distracted by these gadgets.

Want to test your mettle!

You put on the TV. Your favourite movie is being aired. You keep repeating to yourself—I will just watch the beginning of this movie. As you sit down in front of the TV, the beginning takes you halfway through and the end is not very far either. Net result—you end up losing many precious hours of study, not to mention the strained eyes and headache.

So what should be the solution?

Delay this urge by some time, so that you get some time to regain control. If you think you cannot do it yourself, ask someone to stop you when the urge takes over. And that someone can be none other than your own will-power.

*You can make your will-power stronger by using the Placard technique. It is very simple, actually. Make a few cardboard placards of 4' by 4' that say that you are not supposed to indulge in this activity.*

*Suppose you want to stay away from TV, then write down the message in bold letters mentioning the date till you have been prohibited.*

*'NO TV FOR ARCHANA TILL 6$^{TH}$ APRIL'*

*Place this placard on the TV so that you can see it clearly whenever you approach it. The result is that as soon as you approach the TV, you read the placard. It acts as a reminder and your will-power takes over. Force yourself to do it once or twice. Soon you will see dramatic results. You will actually start enjoying not putting on the TV. It is the high that you get out of being 'in control' of things. The thrill is unbeatable.*

# Learning time management

***Shruti had to prepare a project report, which was to be submitted during her board practical exam. The teacher allotted different topics to the whole class much in advance. Most of the children completed their projects well within time. Shruti, however, kept delaying the project on some pretext or the other till only two days were left for the practical exam. Now was the time to take drastic measures. She frantically searched for the matter, wrote the fifteen pages of report in an almost illegible handwriting and made some quick diagrams which were pathetic. This consumed so much of her time that she could not prepare for the viva-voce and other experiments. Her practical exam was a fiasco. If only she had completed her report in time......***

*Each man is the designer of his own fate.*

At some point of time in life, you too must have experienced the predicament Shruti faced. We all make the mistake of taking time lightly and then repenting later.

Just imagine, there is a bank that credited you with Rs. 86,400 every morning with a promise that it's all yours. But there is one condition attached to it—at the end of the day, whatever balance is left will simply be taken away. What would you do in such a case. Obviously, spend the entire amount wisely and make full use of the money. This is what we must do with all the time we have. Each day has 86,400 seconds that you can use as you like. Now it is up to you whether you make full use of each moment and gain from it or waste away most of it.

*Important jobs are tiny till they become urgent and turn into monsters. So kill the monster while it is still small.*

Once you understand the importance of time and how to use it successfully, you will be an expert in time management. The essence of time management lies in devoting maximum time to the important tasks which may turn into urgent tasks tomorrow if not dealt in time. So, if you complete all your important tasks on time, there will be no urgent tasks left for tomorrow and you may use your spare time in fun activities which are neither urgent nor important but refreshing.

Make a table like this and find out how you categorise things in your schedule. It will also give you a fair idea of how usefully you are spending your precious 86,400 seconds every day.

| *Time* | *Activity* | *Category (urgent, important, leisure)* |
|---|---|---|
| 7-8 am | Freshen up, have bath, breakfast | Important |
| 10-11 am | Going through notes for the next days test | Urgent |
| 5-6 pm | Playing badminton | Leisure |
| | | |
| | | |

## Let's grill you

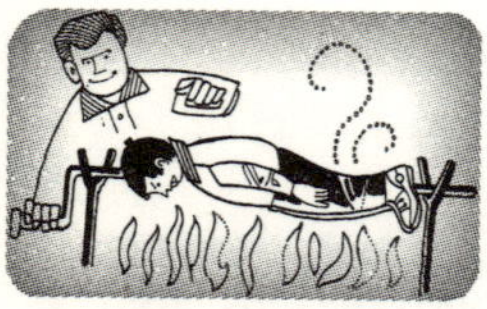

**Using the marking key, categorise the following tasks into A,B,C,D.**

**A - Urgent and important**

**B - Urgent but not important**

**C - Important but not urgent**

**D - Neither urgent nor important**

1. Preparing project report which you have to submit in a month's time.
2. Answering the doorbell.
3. Watching television.

4. Preparing for class test tomorrow.
5. Chatting on phone.
6. Buying a gift for friend's birthday which falls tomorrow.
7. Making notes for the chapter you studied in school today.
8. Completing activity file for tomorrow's practical exam.

**Answers**

**A - 4,8**

**B - 2,6**

**C - 1,7**

**D - 3,5**

If all your answers are correct, then you understand the difference between urgent and important tasks. With a little effort on your part, you can easily manage your time. Time management comes naturally to you.

***Just Chill***

How to get more done in a day—

Every morning, write down the six most important things you want to do on that day. Start doing them one after the other. Keep adding more with each passing day. Soon you will realise that you are covering much more in a day than ever before.

# S Q 3 R—a time-tested technique

***Rani used to put in many hours of study. She would make notes on time and learn them also. Still she always got average marks in exams. She felt very disheartened till one day her cousin Manika came to her house. Manika understood her problem. She taught Rani how to study with SQ3R technique. Rani stood second in her class that year.***

*Survey, Question, Read, Recall and Revise are the five commandments of SQ3R.*

We all keep asking our friends, peers, elders to give us some magic formula to study effectively. The answer is very simple—**SQ3R**.

You must be wondering what this technique is. SQ3R is a time-tested technique. It helps you increase your grasping power. Many educationists recommend this technique for effective study. The five steps in this formula are—

1. **Survey – get to know what you need to learn.**

   You must survey the material you have to read by using speed reading technique (we shall come to it in the following chapters). This helps your mind to get in the mode of absorbing information. It also creates a good background for the next step.

2. **Question – why, how, where and when of information.**

   Now set your objectives by asking questions about the topic. Especially ask questions about what you feel is relevant and important.

*Obstacles are those frightful things you see when you take your eyes off your goal.*

3. **Read – as much as you can on the matter, the more the better.**

   After you have asked the question, you need to search for the answers. So keeping the questions in your mind, set out on a reading mission. Read very attentively and with full focus. You may also take notes while reading.

**4. Recall – by reciting.**

Repetition helps retention of information. It hammers the material in your memory. After reading the material and making notes of the same, you need to speak out loudly, at least the points which you have jotted down so painstakingly. What happens now is that when you hear the matter, you will learn it quickly. hearing after writing gives a double effect and it will be etched in your memory forever.

**5. Revise – periodic revision helps you learn better.**

The final and the most important step is to revise your material using fast revision technique. This makes sure that the matter goes to your permanent memory from temporary memory.

Try out this fundamental technique of effective study on anything new you are going to study and see the difference.

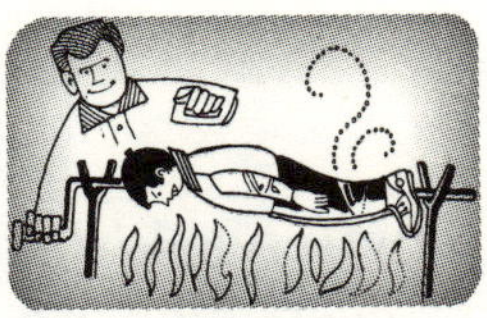

## Let's grill you

**Pick out the right choice.**

***Marking key***

Give (2) marks for each 'a' answer and (1) mark for each 'b' answer.

**Marks**

1. When you read a passage that you do not find very interesting, you— a/b ☐
   a. read each and every word.
   b. just glance at it and move on.
2. While making notes, you— a/b ☐
   a. keep the course book and reference books open.
   b. rely on your memory and finish the work quickly.

3. When you go to the library, you read a/b ☐
   a. books related to your course.
   b. story books, magazines etc.
4. After making notes, you a/b ☐
   a. keep revising them at different intervals.
   b. keep them aside till some later date.
5. When you try to learn a chapter, you a/b ☐
   a. read aloud.
   b. read it silently for the fear of disturbing others. ☐

### *Interpretation*

- **7 and above :** You are on your way to success. You have understood the SQ3R and you implement it successfully in your study schedule.
- **6 and below :** You need to improvise on your study techniques as they are not giving you the right output. You need to devote more time and efforts to your studies to achieve success in your exams.

### *Just Chill*

Challenge yourself to a whole day without saying anything. Write lists but do not contact anyone else verbally. Don't even pick up phones or answer the doorbell. Soon you will realise how and what you think when normal modes of communication have been taken away from you.

# Speed reading and writing (SR&W)

***Shashank's mother worked in an office. She came home late in the evening. After coming from school, Shashank would spend most of his time watching cartoons on TV. As he grew up, he switched to playing computer games in his spare time. His reading and writing skills were limited to his school work and doing home work. He was a bright child, so he managed to fare average in his exams, causing no worry to his parents. It so happened that his mother met with an accident and fractured her leg. She was forced to take leave for six weeks. It was during this period she realised how slow her son was in reading and writing. He just could not concentrate on his books for more than ten minutes. She gave all her time to him now and taught him the importance of speed reading and writing. After some practice, Shashank found his grades improving. He felt on top of the world when he stood first in his class test.***

*The best way to improve your language skills is to use the language as often as possible.*

**Speed reading**

One of the best ways to save time is to do speed reading. When you read fast you get a rough idea of what you are reading. But how to read faster. You begin by using your finger. You need to train your eyes initially to follow your finger. Move your finger as your read. Do this for at least 10 minutes and then start increasing the speed of your finger. As you increase the speed further, soon there will be no need to take the finger from one end to the other. You will just be able to keep it in the centre of the lines. You will still be able to read faster. Remember, speed reading is not an alternative to normal reading, but it is actually an exercise to make normal reading more effective.

*Mind, like muscle, is developed by use.*

## Speed writing

Most people hesitate to write, fearing that they may not be able to do well. But the truth is that everyone can write well, provided one is aware of the simple techniques of writing.

- Relax while writing.
- Note down all the points which you would like to emphasise on rough paper.
- Mark them in your order of preference.
- Make the introduction attractive so as to arouse the interest of the reader.
- String common points into a paragraph and then proceed logically.
- Use simple words with short sentences.
- Your message should be clear, concise, convincing and interesting to the reader.
- The more you write, the faster and efficient you become in your writing skills.

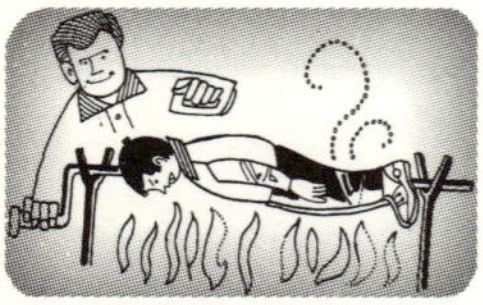

## Let's grill you

**A.** Read this passage of 50 words using speed reading technique and check your speed.

**Writing in itself is a technique which one learns only through practice. It involves knowledge of the language, good communication skills and the ability to think in terms of how others will interpret the words and expressions used. Observe the work of others. Adapt ideas to suit your own style.**

- If you manage to read this passage in 5 seconds, then your average speed comes to 600 wpm, which is a decent speed.

- If you take 10 seconds, then your speed is 300 wpm, which is less than average. You need to improve it.
- Reading this passage in less than 5 seconds puts you in the category of fast readers.

**B.** Write the above passage in your own words and style. You may improvise by using your own ideas. You may increase the word count up to 75 words.

***Just Chill***

Don't slump. Sit straight.

Give your internal organs room to spread and function in the optimum space they need and deserve. Your body will be able to detox effectively leaving you feeling healthy and refreshed.

# Fast revision technique (FRT)

***You are pushing a car up a slope. You push it up to two thirds of the slope and then you pause to take rest without applying any brakes. You take such a long break that you do not even realise that the car has rolled back to the starting point. As you go back to the starting point and push the car again, you will have to spend extra energy to take the car beyond that point.***

***If you continue that way, it will require a Herculean effort to reach the top end of the slope!***

***Do you get the point?!***

Human mind has the tendency to lose information. It works on the simple principle of data in memory and recollection for the brain. Either use your memory or lose the data. If the information you have grasped has no immediate use, it will be lost from the current memory. This does not mean that it will be totally erased. In fact, the mind loses as much as 75% of the learnt matter by the following day if it is not revised.

Brain works on a simple principle – use it or lose it.

Now what could be the solution? The solution is very simple. Do not take such long breaks. Unfortunately, this is the biggest mistake we all often commit with regard to our studies. We study something by heart and then bury it away hoping to retrieve it at a later date. But when we try to get it back after a month or so, we are sadly surprised to find that most of it is lost. FRT helps you keep your memory at a constant level.

There is nothing as powerful as truth, brain and speed.

**FRT is a simple method of frequent revision**

- Revise what you have learnt on that day itself.
- Clear all the doubts at that moment.
- At the end of the week, go through it again.
- Once again, at the end of the month, revise it.
- Keep doing it every month.

Revision just means speed reading through the chapter, followed by recollection. If this is followed religiously, you will be amazed to see the impact—you will develop an astonishingly sharp memory which will be a matter of envy for all your peers.

It is very simple to monitor your FRT. Just have a checklist for each subject in this manner and see how you fare.

**FRT Checklist**

**Subject** - ..................

| Chapter | First revision soon after lecture | Second revision on the next day | Third revision after a week | Fourth revision after a month | Fifth revision after three months |
|---|---|---|---|---|---|
| | | | | | |
| | | | | | |
| | | | | | |
| | | | | | |
| | | | | | |
| | | | | | |

## Let's grill you

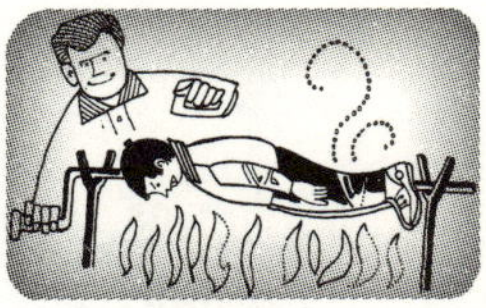

**Fill in the above sheet at random for any two subjects which you think you have prepared.**

- If all the columns have been ticked, then you need not fill this chart anymore because you are already using FRT and you are obviously getting good grades.
- If you have not ticked most of the columns, then start using FRT now and see your grades soar. It is never too late to begin.

# Teach me, teach you

***Sumita sat sulking in her room. Her three friends had gathered at Richa's house for group study but her mother refused to send her there. When she insisted, her mother scolded her by reminding how they all behaved last week when they had got together at Sumita's place for group study. Sumita remembered clearly. That day their group study had started off well. But after fifteen minutes of intense group discussion, someone said something funny and they all started laughing. Their pace was lost and somehow they never got it back on track. The group study ended there and all they did for the next hour was chat, laugh and have fun. Sumita's mother was a witness to all that and fearing its repetition again, she refused to send Sumita for group study to her friend's house.***

*Group study works for those who study with a sincere and disciplined mind.*

To most of us, the concept of group study seems to be a waste of time. But if the group consists of sincere members, then this is one of the best ways to study. When a group of around 4-5 students study the same subject together, we call it group study. There are three conditions which need to be fulfilled in order to make group study a success.

- The place of study should be **without distraction**
- The members should be **sincere**
- They should all **agree** to the subject and topic to study

*Tough times don't last, tough people do.*

**Teach me, teach you** is the best technique in group study. Whenever you want to learn a particular chapter, just divide it into different sections. Each member should be assigned a section. Now it is the responsibility of that member to explain that part to the rest of the group. A thorough reading of the section, looking up in the dictionary for the meanings of the difficult words, and searching for more text on the matter makes you thorough in that section. When you explain it to your friends, it gets etched in your memory. The competition between the members as to who could explain better, motivates all the members to work hard.

**Group study has many virtues**

- Group discussions help in learning new views and ideas
- Majority of doubts are solved by others, instantly
- You learn many valuable tips
- Healthy competition is beneficial for overall development
- You learn more in less time

## Let's grill you

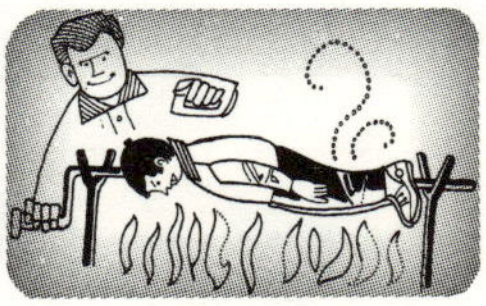

**Answer these questions in 'Yes' or 'No' to find out whether your group studies are effective or not.**

1. You have a group of five friends who sincerely believe in studying together. Yes/No
2. You prefer to assemble in a public park for group study. Yes/No
3. During group study, you have a group leader who is responsible for maintaining the decorum of the group. Yes/No
4. Your study group sits together but studies subjects of their own choice irrespective of what the others are doing. Yes/No
5. You have received valuable tips from your friends during group study. Yes/No
6. You find group study a lot of fun where you joke, laugh, and make fun of all your teachers. Yes/No

### *Interpretation*

- If the answers of 1, 3, and 5 are in 'Yes' and 2, 4, and 6 are in 'No', then you are taking full advantage of group study. The benefits you derive from this method are far greater than studying alone.
- But if your answers are vice versa, then you are just having fun. You while away your precious time chatting and gossiping. You discuss everything under the sun except for one thing, and that's studies. Begin your group study on a more serious note and see the difference in your performance.

### *Just Chill*

When your friends come over for a session of group study, fill the gaps with delicious snacks which are nutritious as well as delicious.

This will renew your energy levels and replenish your brainpower.

Sutra 7

# Practise for Perfection

***Before writing the final exams, we all have to go through various practice sessions including tests and revisions. Taking practice tests lightly is a common mistake we all commit. Our attitude towards these tests is—'Why slog so hard, they are just class tests. They do not even count in our report cards.' Apparently, the marks that you score in revision tests may not count in the final score but they do make a difference. They help you assess your abilities and hard work put in by you. Giving them your best shot is equally important because you will write the same answers in your final exams that you have revised or practiced in your practice tests. If you have been taking it easy in your tests, you will do the same in your examinations too.***

Most of us are in the habit of taking tests lightly. But there are two major disasters that can occur because of such an attitude:

- Firstly, you will never know your true potential because you will always tend to believe that you can do much better than this.

- Secondly, you will surely perform in the finals just the way you have been consistently doing in your tests.

So the attitude of 'saving your best for the last' does not work here. You have simply not practised to be the best. You see, there is no logic in just giving tests for the heck of it. Constant and dedicated practice is the secret of achievers. Practise for perfection and you will get perfect results.

Remember, practice will make you perfect, provided that practice is perfect itself.

# Building a vocabulary

***Whenever Swati wrote her exams, she could not finish it on time because she had to tax her brains to find the right word. For the same reason, she was very slow while doing her homework or writing in the class. Her mother took her to a psychologist who examined her and put her through some IQ tests. The tests showed that she had average IQ but her vocabulary was very poor. She was advised to work on building up her vocabulary.***

*A good vocabulary is to a student what ammunition is to a soldier - the more you have, the stronger you feel.*

We need to communicate through a language. English continues to be the most popular language across the world. By knowing English, you can find your way almost anywhere in the world. Competitive exams like **MBA, CAT, BMS, TOEFL** test your vocabulary. So it is a wise decision to invest in a good vocabulary for a good future. English language has around two million words. You cannot expect to learn all of them, but having a good vocabulary has its advantages.

There are two kinds of vocabulary in each of us—

**Receptive Vocabulary** – words that you understand when you hear or read them.

**Active Vocabulary** – words you use to express yourself when you speak or write.

By reducing the gap between receptive and active vocabulary, you can strengthen your word power.

*A child's mind is like a bank. What you put in you get back with interest after a few years.*

Many people believe that reading enhances vocabulary. It does, but there is a condition attached to it. As soon as you come across a new word, make sure to look up its meaning in the dictionary rather than assuming it. Once you know the meaning of that word, try to use it in your normal course of conversation. The more you use that word, the sooner it will become a part of your vocabulary.

Here are some tips on how to build up your vocabulary:

- Take interest in words.
- Have a dictionary as your constant companion.
- Do not hesitate to check any word that is not very clear to you.
- Try to learn new words everyday.
- Make a note of these words and review them periodically.
- Buying a Thesaurus or a book of synonyms and antonyms is a good investment. They carry a wide range of words having similar meaning, with varying shades to each of them.
- Always keep in mind that words are the tools of precise communication.

## Let's grill you

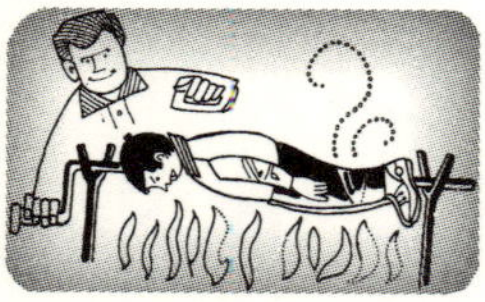

**While taking this test, you will not consult the dictionary or take help from your elders.**

***Marking key***

Give (1) mark for each correct answer and judge your vocabulary.

1. Write meanings of these words—
   Casual – ...............
   Heredity – .............
   Catastrophe – ..........
   Impulsive – .....................
2. English language has many words that sound similar but have different meanings. Write the meanings of these words—

| | |
|---|---|
| Decent | descent |
| Bail | bale |
| Flare | flair |
| Deer | dear |

3. These words not only sound similar, they also share the same spelling. Write their meanings—

| | |
|---|---|
| Dear | dear |
| Bear | bear |
| Letter | letter |
| Right | right |

4. All of you may be familiar with punctuation marks. Let's see how many you can recognise—

(,)......... (;)......... (:)......... (!).........

(?)......... (-)......... (" ").........( ' )...........

***Interpretation***

15-20 : Very good

8-14 : Fair

0-7 : Need improvement

**Ans.** (1) unconcerned; inherited traits; great disaster; rash

(2) polite – fall; surety – bundle; blaze – style; an animal – beloved.

(3) beloved – expensive; an animal – tolerate; a written document – an alphabet; correct – entitled to.

(4) comma; semi colon; colon; exclamation mark; question mark; hyphen; quotation marks; apostrophe.

# Improving handwriting

***Ravi showed a note from his teacher to his mother saying that he needs to do one page of cursive writing everyday. Cursive writing—in class X, it was unthinkable! Practising handwriting is for small children. When Ravi's mother contacted the teacher, she showed her Ravi's answer sheets. In his hurry to complete the paper, Ravi wrote all his answers in an almost illegible handwriting. Regular practice was the only solution for improving the style and speed of his handwriting.***

*Handwriting is an art open to any amateur, for the delight he gets from it himself and the further pleasure he gives to others.*

Handwriting links you to the examiner. Let me put it this way. The only link between you and the examiner who is going to decide your destiny is your answer copy. And your answers are written in your handwriting. So your handwriting becomes a mirror of your personality.

If you receive a gift, wrapped nicely in glittering paper with ribbons tied all around, you feel happy. If you receive the same gift without the wrapping and in a shabby poly bag, you would definitely rate the gift much lower than the wrapped one. A gift wrapper makes the gift attractive and receivable. Your handwriting is what the wrapper is to the gift. It is a medium to put your message across. A good handwriting gives a pleasing effect and gets you pleasing marks.

*When you know you have done all that is possible in any situation, then the problem is no longer yours.*

Here are some important things you should remember while writing.

- Write neatly.
- Stick to the line you write on. Do not shuffle between the lines.
- Form your alphabets well.
- They should be of uniform height. The small alphabets should be of same height and the tall ones should also reach to a uniform height.
- Spacing is a very important tool of handwriting.

- Provide enough space between words. This gives your handwriting a good impression and it makes your answers seem longer than they really are.
- Neatness in presentation is equally important.

To practise and improve handwriting and neatness, an ideal time is when you prepare notes. Spend time over them. They will give you an opportunity to write legibly and neatly. Besides, if they are written clearly, you will find it a pleasure to go through them when you need to make revisions just before exams.

## Let's grill you

**How important is handwriting to you? Assess it by answering these questions:**

1. Do you write neatly and legibly?
2. Do you have good knowledge of the language you communicate in?
3. Can you write your answers neatly without making changes?
4. Do you feel you are getting marks as per your studies?
5. Can you write neatly even during speed writing?

### *Marking key*

- If most or all your answers are in the affirmative (Yes), then you need not worry. You have a good handwriting and you need not practise it out of the way. But work hard to keep it that way by sticking to your style and formation of words.
- If most or all your answers are in the negative (No), then you need to practise handwriting. It does not take long to get your handwriting back in shape. I assure you, then you will not want to lose it. Believe me, once there, you will stick to it.

## Being precise and compact

***Nidhi believed in writing long answers. Since it took time, she would hurriedly go on writing her paper during exams. When she joined her new school in class X, she continued with the same practice. Her friends were amazed how she could fill sheets after sheets in the exams whereas they barely managed to take one or two supplementary sheets. When the results were declared Nidhi was surprised that she got much less marks in English than she had expected. She took her paper to her teacher and demanded an explanation. The teacher told her that filling up sheets did not add up to marks. She was supposed to write her answers in the given word limit. She even showed her the question paper where the word limit was clearly mentioned. In short, she must learn to be precise and to the point, otherwise her marks would be deducted.***

*The ability to communicate well overshadows all the other skills.*

There is, no doubt, a sense of urgency in the students while answering questions. It is but natural that we would like to use as much time for writing as possible. But while doing this we tend to make a very expensive mistake—not reading the questions properly.

Whenever you see a question, your mind scans it for something similar—like a word or a phrase. The moment you locate it, you immediately jump to answer it. Many a times, your answer may not be what has been asked in the question. In this way, you irritate the examiner and lose marks.

*Great things are not done by an impulse but by a series of small things brought together.*

Another common mistake is that you do not read the various parts of a question. You answer the first part and move on to the next question. This again makes you lose marks.

The solution to this problem is very simple. Pay full attention to your question. Reread it and make sure what is being asked in the question. Also read the instructions carefully. All this will help you frame the correct answer to the question. Always remember to answer what is asked.

Being compact and precise has its advantages. A precise answer should have the right terms, key words and graphics. This does not put unnecessary burden on the examiner to search for the key words. It also saves you time which you may use in revising your paper at the end of it.

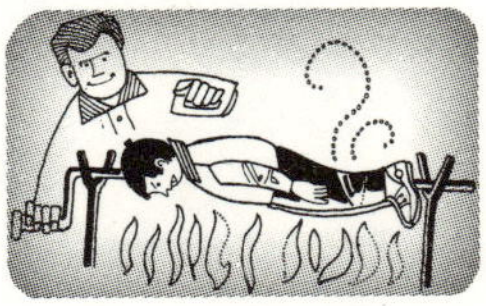

## Let's grill you

**Answer these questions.**

1. Write two words from this chapter which signify its importance. There is no need to elaborate on them.

2. 'One is not born with communication skills. They are learnt.' Write a paragraph on this topic in not more than 50 words.

3. Write the first four lines of the national anthem. Also, write the name of its poet.

4. What do Adolf Hitler, Mussolini, Idi Amin and Saddam Hussain have in common? Write a paragraph in not more than 50 words.

If you have answered all the questions accurately and within their limits, if they are compact and precise, then you may rest assured that you are on the right path.

***Just Chill***

Challenge your comfort zone and see how brilliant you feel once you have achieved something you never dreamt possible.

# Writing an examiner-friendly paper

***When Sheela sat down to check the examination papers, she was in a good mood and wanted to give good grades to all the students. As she went through the papers, she found that most of the students had written the answers haphazardly. Some had even forgotten to write the question number. Some of them attempted a question in two parts and that too at different ends of the paper. Some had not tied their supplementary sheets in the right order, so she had to spend unnecessary time searching for their answers here and there. After checking five or six such papers, she felt so tired that she put the bunch down. She had lost her enthusiasm and was in a bad mood now.***

*Why did MS Windows replace MS DOS ? It was more user-friendly.*

No examiner ever spends more than a few minutes on the paper. A question paper that is written in three hours is thus examined in a few minutes. In these few minutes, the entire future of the student gets decided. How can you turn the destiny in your favour? By making your paper examiner-friendly. The idea is to make it as easy for the examiner as possible to read your answers – and of course, give marks.

You must know that each examiner is given something called the model answers. The examiners generally don't read your answers word to word. They match how similar your answer is with the model one (except the language papers), and allot marks accordingly. As a paper moves smoothly, the examiner too gets into a positive mode and your chances of scoring well become brighter.

*Our mind is a jungle but proper education can turn it into a garden.*

**There are a few tips which you must remember while writing an examiner-friendly paper—**

- Your presentation should be good.
- Try to attempt the questions exactly in the same way as written in the question paper.

This helps the examiner identify the answer immediately and he recognises the set pattern.

- Your answers in subjects like Mathematics and Physics shuld be boxed for immediate identification.
- Never attempt a question in two parts—and that too at different ends of the paper.
- Tie your supplementary sheets in the right order.
- Start each answer on a fresh page.
- Make sure your handwriting is legible with sufficient spacing between the words.
- There should be minimum cutting on the paper. It should look neat.
- Structure your answers properly.
- Use capital letters, bullets and underlining as tools to attract attention to important points.
- If you have used any page for rough work, it, should be crossed and clearly marked 'Rough Work'.

Remember, all this will help the examiner, who in turn will then help you get good grades.

## Let's grill you

It's time to get your answer papers evaluated to check as to how examiner-friendly they are.

Take a model paper of any subject (except the language papers).

Attempt it first in your own style.

Attempt a similar paper a second time after a gap of a few days in an examiner-friendly style.

Get both the papers checked by the same teacher. Request your teacher to rate each of your answer papers according to a model list as shown below. Then add up your marks and see the difference in marks.

| Criteria | Paper written in your own style | Examiner-friendly paper |
|---|---|---|
| Presentation | | |
| Vocabulary | | |
| Accuracy | | |
| Handwriting | | |
| Question Nos. | | |
| Others | | |
| Total marks - | | |

***Just Chill***

If something bad happens, think of five steps to turn it into something good by turning negative into positive.

Suppose you missed your school bus—

- You can either walk or ride a cycle and enjoy the cool breeze.
- The brisk walk/cycling will give you the required exercise for the day.
- You may enjoy nature.
- You managed to escape the dust/smoke.
- You do not have to fight for a seat in the bus.

Sutra 8

# An Edge Over Others

***The struggle for existence is present in every sphere of life. It is the survival of the fittest. Same is the case with exams also. Exams are one way of selecting the fittest students for moving ahead in life. That is the reason why you see competitive exams of different kinds all over. All youngsters need to appear in exams to prove their worth.***

***To venture ahead of others, it is imperative that you set goals and learn a little more than others. You must adopt better habits and develop skills which give you an edge. The purpose is not merely to face the world. You need to forge ahead. Do not assume others to be any less than you. All that you need is to have confidence in your abilities and a plan which shall help you emerge a winner. Devise a strategy to be more competitive and surge ahead of others.***

# Be inquisitive in your approach

***Let me tell you a story of the twin brothers, Tarun and Varun. Since childhood, Tarun would ask innumerable questions and get reprimanded. Observing his twin brother being scolded for asking questions, Varun learnt to keep quiet and hardly ever put across any query. Tarun, however, refused to take the hint and kept on persisting till he was totally satisfied. Tarun was mocked at by the whole class, teachers scorned at him, but he remained adamant. Many a times he was sent out for disturbing the class by his excessive questioning. But everyone was pleasantly surprised when Tarun scored highest in his board exams while Varun got average marks.***

*He who asks questions may seem a fool for once, but he who does not, remains a fool for life.*

One of the most powerful tools a student has is an inquisitive mind. If you want to have an edge over others, then asking questions will help you learn. Look at any kid—how curious he is about everything around him. It is this curiosity which makes him learn. Sadly, we lose curiosity as we grow up. It is not as if we know everything by then. It is only that the urge to learn has been curbed by others who make fun or do not give due importance to our queries. But this is one attitude one must guard against.

As you grow up, you stop asking about your doubts in the open for fear of embarrassment. However, you must keep one thing in mind that if you have a doubt, surely there are others who have the same doubt but lack the courage to stand up in front of the whole class and ask the teacher. Would you believe, that in the heart of hearts, each one of them would be praying that someone else ask the doubt. When you are the saviour, they will surely praise your guts, silently.

*Inquisitiveness is our armour and it can raise us to an altitude where the stones hurled at us won't hurt us.*

To be admired by them, the quality of questions that you ask are also very important. If you feel your doubt is unique or sort of silly, consult the teacher in private. In this way, you will save yourself embarrassment and will not feel discouraged. Compete with your friends in asking questions. Just make sure that your questions are not stupid, else you will be in trouble.

Any teacher appreciates a student who is curious enough to ask. The only way to seek help is by asking.

Remember the story of Alladin who found a genie. Alladin had three wishes—but to fulfil them, he had to ASK the genie. So now you see the importance of asking questions.

## Let's grill you

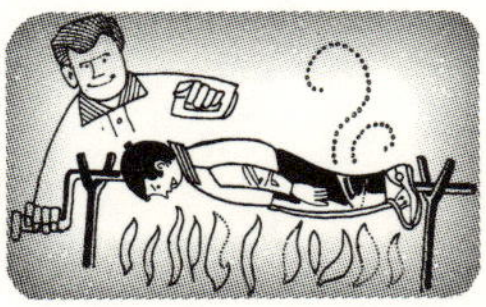

**Read these questions and mark those you feel would sound stupid.**

1. Sir, could you please explain the fifth paragraph on page 121 again? ☐
2. Sir, I was minding the class when you taught this chapter. Can we do the chapter again? ☐
3. Sir, you explained this theorem to Shashi, Ruchit and Sanjay individually. Why can't you explain it to me? ☐
4. Sir, that part where you derive the formula is not clear to all of us. Could you please repeat it for us? ☐
5. Sir, it may be the tenth time that you are explaining this formula to me, but what can I do if your way of teaching is beyond my comprehension? ☐

**Answers**

1 and 4 are the questions which are sensible enough for a student to ask. They give the impression of an inquisitive mind. Questions 2, 3, and 5 are the questions which are not asked out of curiosity but for the sake of it.

If you have deduced the above results correctly, then you have a fair idea of how to ask good questions in class. You have an inquisitive mind.

But if your results are different from ours, then you are merely having fun in the class at the expense of your teacher or fellow students. Give up this habit. Instead of crying wolf, try to catch it by the tail.

## Take initiative, have belief

***Once, a doctor gave his patient six pills to be taken within two days, for cold and cough. He asked him to come for a check-up again. The patient came back after two days but his health had not improved. The doctor asked him, "Did you take the medicine I gave you?" The patient sheepishly replied, "They are in my pocket."***

If you do not want to change or take initiative, even God cannot help you. And if you take the initiative, then you do not need anybody's help. The world's most powerful weapon will be of no use if it is not put to use. To put something to use, you must take initiative. You must learn to live in the present. This is the time to change. Why keep postponing things till eternity? This is the time to take the first step. Wake up! Grab the opportunities. Opportunities do not come knocking at your door every day. Have belief in your abilities and change for the better. Even if a small chunk of this thought is applied, it will bring major changes in your life. But the keyword is initiative—it needs to be applied.

Initiative comes with a belief in your abilities. All the winners have a trait in common—they create beliefs. They believe that they can win. Once a belief is formed, subsequent experiences will be more or less fitting into that mould.

It is the same with failing. If you fail once, you form a negative belief about your experience. You go on failing thereafter because subconsciously, you have convinced yourself that you are a failure in life. So keep a positive belief, it will produce positive results.

> *We must accept finite disappointment. But we must never lose infinite hope.*

Have you ever seen an elephant tied with a rope. If the elephant is strong enough to lift heavy logs, don't you think it is capable of breaking that piece of rope also. It certainly is, still it won't break the rope to run free. Why? Because when the elephant was a baby, the mahout first tied it to the rope. At that time, the elephant was not strong enough to break the rope. It tried and tried, but could not succeed. So the elephant formed a belief that it was not possible to break the rope. Isn't it interesting?

But sadly, we all do the same thing. So we all need to come out of our beliefs and take initiative to succeed in life, to be able to form newer and more positive beliefs.

*You are what you think you are.*

## Let's grill you

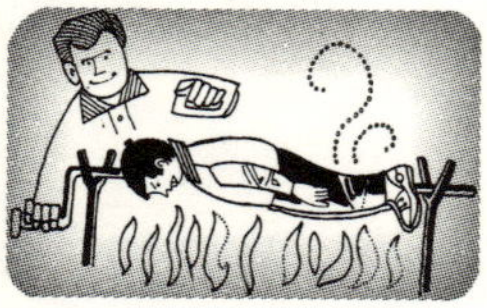

**Given below are two lists with ten general beliefs that most of us form in everyday life. Tick (✓) the ones you also believe in.**

**A.**

1. I am no good.
2. I am a loser.
3. Catastrophe follows me everywhere.
4. I am highly accident-prone.
5. I am just an average student.
6. My luck ditches me at the most inappropriate moment.
7. I am living the worst life on this earth.
8. Everyone is out to put me down.
9. My own people do not value me.
10. Life is a drag.

**B.**

1. I am as good as any other student in my class.
2. I am an achiever.
3. My hard work is my strength.

4. Accidents are a part of life.
5. I am the best.
6. My luck is with me.
7. I am thankful to God for giving me this life.
8. We are all equals.
9. I am the apple of my parents' life.
10. Life is beautiful.

### *Interpretation*

- If you have ticked most of the beliefs in list A and some in list B, then you need to strengthen your beliefs more. Your beliefs will boost your confidence. Renewed confidence will fill you with the power to take initiative.
- If most of your beliefs belong to list B, then you are on the right track. Having faith in your abilities is the first step towards success.

### *Just Chill*

Laughter is prayer. Just the touch of laughter can make life something worth living. Laughter brings strength. If you can laugh, you have learnt how to pray.

So laugh off your woes and fill yourself with joy and fun.

# Follow reserve hour technique

***Whenever Sandhya made a timetable, she could not follow it. Either her study hours would shrink by a quarter of an hour; or her sleeping time would stretch to another extra hour; or her leisure hour would seem endless. Even if she tried to follow it religiously, somehow it would not work out. Finally, she felt frustrated and dumped it.***

*Reserve hour is that hidden hour of your day which provides for contingencies.*

Not only Sandhya, many students face this problem. Sir Parkinson gave a very significant law about work—**Work has a tendency to expand and occupy the available time.** So, if you provide one hour for a job which would ordinarily take half an hour, you will end up using all the time for it.

Time has a very big disadvantage. It does not wait for anyone. If you have been following a timetable in daily routine, you would have noticed that as the activities of the day go on, their preset time gets delayed. This affects all the activities after that and ultimately your timetable loses its significance. To make it more clear to you, I will give you an example—suppose you have set your afternoon nap hours from 3-4 pm, and two hours after that, i.e., 4-6 pm has been allotted for playing. Since you overslept, you got up late and went to play at 5 pm instead of 4 pm which means you will return at 7 pm instead of 6 pm and start studies late. Since you need to accommodate your TV programme which comes at a fixed hour, you cut down on your study hour. In fact, in such cases the least pleasurable activities get axed. So whenever you are short on time, the general tendency is to cut out the study part of it.

To handle this problem, a very simple technique has been evolved which can make a timetable more effective. It is called the **Reserve Hour Technique.** When you plan your day in the morning, you generally tend to allocate all the time by keeping one activity immediately after another. There are two ways to avoid this problem—

- Start each activity some time later than when it normally would. Thus, even if the previous activity takes up more time, you will be in a comfortable position.
- Leave atleast one hour free in the day where you assign no task at all. This hour can be in the middle of the day or at the end, so that all the time lost during the day may be adjusted in this hour. Never commit the mistake of putting this hour at the start of the day. If the tasks overlap the allocated time, the reserve hour acts as a buffer and keeps your timetable intact. But on the other hand, if luckily your hour remains free, you can use it to do anything you want.

*Education is the ability to use what you have learnt to be better today, than what you were yesterday.*

Now you see the importance of allotting this reserve hour. It is not only a real time-saver, it is a life-saver too. It takes away the tension and stress of sticking strictly to schedules each day.

# Let's grill you

Given below is the format of two schedules where you have to allot the time and activities. Prepare one with reserve hour, and the other one by providing extra time to each activity.

| Schedule 1 | Time | Activity |
|---|---|---|
| | | |
| | | |
| | | |
| | | |
| | | Reserve hour |
| | | |
| | | |
| | | |

| Schedule 2 | Time | Extra time | Activity |
|---|---|---|---|
| | | | |
| | | | |
| | | | |

Try both the timetables for a week each, and find out which one suits you better.

Also check what you did in the reserve hour.

***Just Chill***

Keep your metabolic rate from slumping into very low by eating five smaller meals spread evenly across the day. This will keep a good balance of energy throughout the day, and keep your mind fresh and alert.

## Using reward punishment system

***Yash used to surf the internet for hours on end. When his mother raised an objection, he promised to complete his homework after surfing the net for an hour. But most of the time, this hour stretched to two hours and his studies would suffer. So his mother changed the order of his homework and surfing. Now Yash had to complete his homework first, then only he was allowed to surf the net.***

*Pursuing the principle of Delayed Gratification helps you achieve your target.*

Human mind works on a simple formula—the Pain-Pleasure formula. It seeks pleasure and avoids the pain. Our activities in a typical day comprise of a unique blend. Some of these activities like watching TV, talking to a friend on the phone or reading a book give us pleasure. Others are a little painful—like studies! Most of us have a pleasure-seeking mind which always favours pleasure and procrastinates pain. No wonder, most of our plans of time allocation run into trouble. We pick up the fun activities and indulge in them. The time taken by them expands and we find trouble in fitting the not-so-interesting activities in the remaining time slot. End result—all play and no work!

### Delayed Gratification

*Be nice to people on your way up because you will need them on your way down.*

To combat this problem, use the **Reward Punishment System** which is also called **Delayed Gratification.** The logic is very simple. Just put the pleasurable tasks at the end while you complete the painful tasks, like study, before them. Suppose you want to watch TV for one hour. Then you will allow yourself to watch TV only after you study for one hour. The next hour of study will get you the reward of surfing the internet and so on. That is how you will be able to achieve your targets.

In this whole system, you should keep one thing in mind, that it is you who is going to benefit with this system, so it is your duty to make sure that you do not cheat on this system. It is most likely to happen when you are in the gratification stage. To be fair to yourself, it is important that you distribute the awards rationally—neither with extreme generosity nor with strictness.

Adjust the system to work for you. But make sure you delay gratification. The reward should come after the punishment.

Such is the law of nature. Remember, the fruits come only after the seeds are sown and the work is done. So plan out your reward punishment system with delayed gratification for best results.

## Let's grill you

**Answer these questions.**

**What would you do if—**

1. you had two hours of homework left and your favourite programme on TV starts in an hour's time ........................................................
2. you forgot all about studies and carried on with your leisure activity even after the stipulated time .............................................
3. some guests dropped by and you were asked to entertain them ...................................... ...
4. your best friend called when you were on the last leg of completing your studies before you could receive your reward............................
5. your delayed gratification system fails due to your own weakness of rewarding yourself extremely generously..................................

### *Interpretation*

- You are the best judge in these situations. If you are able to control yourself from extending your rewards more than the stipulated periods, then be rest assured that you have mastered the art of delayed gratification.

### *Just Chill*

For doing something worthwhile, like studying regularly, reward yourself with some innovative ideas—

- Get the latest haircut.
- Buy that T-shirt which you had been postponing for a long time.
- Change your pen.
- Change the direction of the bed and study table in your room.

9

Sutra

# Go Global

Advanced technology has made the world a small place. Countries are much better connected than ever before. However, on the flip side, competition is really tough today. The number and variety of exams that are conducted each year is simply astounding. In fact, there is an entire industry catering to the needs of the students who appear in exams. These study aids help you perform better in exams.

Internet is a great source of information and knowledge that did not exist a few years ago. Not only study material, you can even get information about the forthcoming exams, mock tests and scholarships offered by various national as well as international universities.

So, wake up, come out of your shell, go global. There is a vast world before you. Explore it and attain your destination.

# Log on to the net

***Manish was asked to prepare a project report on heart diseases. He consulted many books and journals in his school library but could not find enough matter. He did not know what to do. His cousin Raghu was also studying in class XII. Manish decided to take his help. He called him up. Raghu told him that he had already completed and submitted his project in school. Raghu told Manish that a lot of matter on any subject was available on the internet. He asked Manish to come over so that they could search the net. Within ten minutes, Manish managed to find enough matter to prepare his project report. Manish was amazed at the wide scope of the net.***

*Explore the wonderful world of internet.*

Gone are the days when students had to depend on the school library or the teacher's notes to get extra information. Computers have entered our world in a big way. Internet is a boon for the students. But how many of us really use the net? We all know about net, and for us net means e-mail, chatting and aimless surfing on contest and dating sites.

There are many sites on the internet that give you plenty of information about your subjects. If you spend 15 minutes on the net and research every lesson that you studied that day, then you will find lots more new information which will make you a scholar in your class. Check it with your teacher whether you may use it in your answer paper. This will make your answers unique and outstanding, especially the science subjects—you can get the latest cutting-edge information from internet. All you need to do is make some efforts with the pure intention of learning.

Remember one simple rule, the more you know something, the greater are the chances that you will like it. If you will know more about your subject, you will start loving it too.

Internet has many sites that give details and ways to study effectively. Universities have online libraries which are a great way to read without spending any money. All the latest information is available at the click of the mouse.

**Some ways in which net can be used—**

- **Search Engines** – on one of the numerous search engines like yahoo or google, write "effective studies" and check out the results.
- **Educational sites** – surf educational sites and check out if they offer online course material. You do not have to pay for it. It is generally free of charge.
- **Research** – search for information about the projects that you wish to prepare. Dig deep enough without getting lost.
- **Counselling** – many sites offer expert opinion to clarify your doubts. Put your queries across to them.
- **Discussion groups** – check with the news-groups and discussion boards. You get to express your opinion and know about others' opinion.
- **E-mail contacts** – collect the e-mail addresses of all your peers and classmates, and start an e-mail group of your own. You can then exchange information, solutions, doubts etc. online.

*What goes around, comes around.*

## Let's grill you

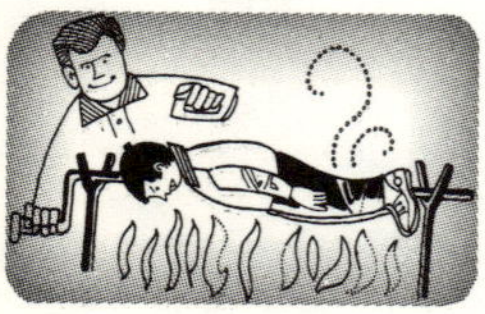

**Given below are a few terms related to internet. Tick the correct meaning and find out how net-friendly you are—**

1. E-mail
   a) a letter with E written on it.
   b) exchanging letters through internet.

2. Search engine
   a) a programme used to search different sites on internet.
   b) it is like a railway engine.
3. surfing
   a) scanning the internet by searching different sites.
   b) using surf excel to clean the computer.
4. site
   a) an address on the internet.
   b) a term in net lingo for eye sight.
5. www
   a) working with wires.
   b) world wide web.

### *Answers*

1(b); 2(a); 3(a); 4(a); 5(b)

### *Interpretation*

- If you have got all the answers correct, then you are no doubt net savvy. So what are you waiting for. The latest breakthroughs in memory and thinking, as well as study techniques, are available on the net. Log in and get updated, else you will be logged out.

  Log on to sites like

  - www.howtostudy.com,
  - www.free-ed.net
  - www.worldwidelearn.com

### *Just Chill*

Wear a colour you have never worn before and see how it makes you feel uplifted and important.

# Reading newspapers

***In Anu's school, it was compulsory for every student to subscribe to the newspaper. They had a special zero period for reading the newspaper in the class. The thought behind the system was very good. But alas, many students did not take this exercise seriously and would spend the entire period gossiping instead of reading the paper. Anu, however, enjoyed reading the newspaper. She loved solving crosswords. There was news of a major earthquake in the paper which she read with interest. The next day, their English teacher asked them to write an essay on earthquakes. The students, including Anu, who had read the previous day's newspaper managed to write the essay in detail while the others found it quite difficult. That day, they realised the importance of reading newspapers.***

*Reading the newspaper is your first step towards awareness.*

Students today have been reduced to being a frog in the well, who considers the well to be its entire world. It does not know what is happening outside the well. For these students their family, friends and school make up their wells. This is not a good practice. As a part of this world, we need to be aware of what is happening around us. And for this, the best way is to read newspapers. Newspapers keep us abreast with the daily happenings around the world. Unfortunately, the readership of newspapers among students is alarmingly low.

Reading the newspaper provides dual benefit. First of all, you get to know the latest happenings in the world and secondly your vocabulary improves. It also improves your comprehension and reading speed—a skill that helps in each and every subject. As you read more, you tend to increase speed, and understand faster. Apart from this, newspapers contain views of the best people of every field. Without much effort, you actually get to share the thoughts of the best in their respective fields.

Newspapers are not all work. They are fun too. You can solve crosswords, Su-doku puzzles, get information about careers and even read the review about a movie before you waste your precious three hours watching it. You even get to know about important notifications regarding exams, syllabi and other topics through newspapers.

*A newspaper is a combo of fun, news, and information.*

Today's leading newspapers carry weekly supplements with different names like Education Times, School Times etc. They are specially written for students. Much useful information about studies can be obtained from these pages.

So start reading newspapers now. They form the base for reading, and improving your general knowledge. If you get into the habit of reading the newspaper now, believe me, it will be very fruitful for you later in life.

## Let's grill you

**If you are a regular reader of a newspaper, then you are obviously familiar with these terms which form an integral part of newspapers. Tick the correct answer.**

1. Classifieds—
   a. talking about various classes in society.
   b. job advertisements.
2. Editorial—
   a. from the editor's desk.
   b. looking for editor's address.
3. Obituary—
   a. celebrating Valentine Day.
   b. notifying death of a person.

4. Matrimonial—
   a. study material for matric level.
   b. column for marriage proposals.
5. Headline—
   a. the main news.
   b. lines on the editor's head.

### *Answers*

1(b); 2(a); 3(b); 4(b); 5(a).

If you are familiar with all these terms, then it is apparent that you are into the newspaper-reading habit. Keep it up.

### *Just Chill*

If your best friend has been working hard or has been through a bad time, then you think of him and decide to give him a treat to cheer him up.

Well, now is the time to be your own best friend.

# Attending career counselling sessions

***All the students of class X were very excited. Their school had arranged a seminar on career counselling. The speaker was a prominent career counsellor. She was coming to their school to guide them. This year was a very crucial year for them. It was a turning point in their lives. They were confused as to what subjects to choose in class XI, because this laid the foundation of their career. The counsellor arrived on time and their seminar began with his speech where he apprised the students about new careers in various fields. Although most of the students had heard of terms like Aeronautical Science, Forensic Science, Biotechnology—they had no idea what exactly these fields offered them. The counsellor clarified all their doubts. The students were glad that they attended this seminar.***

Choosing a career was much simpler till a few decades ago. There was not much competition and choices were also not too many. Today, with so many upcoming fields, there are many options open for the students. However, there is no need to feel disillusioned. Choose the field which you feel interests you most. But before you take the plunge, you need to consider all its aspects. For example, you may wish to be an architect but you may not have the aptitude for drawing at all. In such a case, you will find it hard to pursue your dream career. So be practical in your approach. Consider various options open before you and then go ahead with what you feel is best suited to your temperament.

I know of a girl who was good at writing. She joined BCA on the insistence of her parents, though she wanted to do journalism. She pursued BCA but her heart was still in journalism. During the summer vacation, she got a short term assignment as a newsreader with one of the leading channels. She went ahead with it. The news channel discovered her writing talent when they found her improving the script herself. They offered her a full-time job with their channel. She took it as an opportunity to pursue her dream career and grabbed it immediately. She left her BCA course midway in the bargain. But she was more than happy because now she was doing what she always wanted to do.

However, not all of us can be so lucky. So we have to weigh our options and make our choice carefully. Your school must be organising career festivals called Careerfests. Make it a point to attend them. Leading career counsellors offer advice on the internet and through leading newspapers also. Make full use of it. Do not feel shy in clarifying all the doubts that are lurking in your mind.

*Ask for something you want.*
*Beware–it may result in you getting it.*

### *Just Chill*

Learn to say 'NO'.

If someone wants something that you cannot give—energy, time, brainpower or anything that would make your personal stocks dangerously low—like emotional or physical help—then just say 'NO'.

# Visiting education fairs

***It was Ravindra's dream to do his undergraduate studies from a foreign university. But he did not know how to go about it. One day, he saw an advertisement in the paper about an education fair in the city. He and his friends decided to visit the fair. Ravindra was astounded to see so many foreign universities participating in the fair. He took their addresses and e-mail addresses so that he could contact them at the appropriate time. Some of the universities even enrolled him tentatively. As soon as Ravindra's class XII exams got over, he contacted those universities. He sat for the entrance cum scholarship tests of some universities. Soon enough, he joined a reputed for university which offered him a good scholarship too. His dream was fulfilled.***

*As one lamp lights another it does not grow less. So nobleness enkindles nobleness*

If you read the newspaper, you must have seen the advertisements of education fairs. Sometimes they are jointly held, sometimes they are of individual countries. These fairs are held at a venue which is convenient to everyone. These fairs are mostly genuine. They are conducted directly through the universities. If the fair is organised by an agent, then make sure he is authentic before you waste your time and money there. Some of the universities offer tentative enrolment and charge you a nominal fee. Once you are sure of your ambition and authenticity of the university, then it may prove to be a good investment because then you may get admission on priority basis. You may even get a scholarship which would be on 'first come, first serve' basis.

Education fairs also apprise you about Indian universities which offer various courses and scholarships. Banks, airlines and companies which offer scholarships can be contacted at these fairs and the facilities offered by them can be availed of.

10

Sutra

# Feel Good

*Exams cause anxiety and tension for all. The main reason for such anxiety is the fear of failure. Failure is associated with humiliation and no one likes to be humiliated. Though a little bit of this anxiety is good as it motivates the students to work hard, but an excess of it can create health-related problems. Digestion may be affected. You may become forgetful and suffer from insomnia.*

*All these symptoms vanish if you develop self-confidence as it leads to self-discipline and better preparation.*

*So although your first priority is academic success, recreational activities are equally important to get rid of anxiety and tension.*

*At a time when everything is becoming instant in our world, students also look for instant relief methods. They look for drugs which can relieve the anxiety and tension associated with exams. But this is definitely not advisable as such usage leads to drug abuse and addiction.*

*Instead, deep breathing exercises, outdoor games, meditation and prayers help relieve anxiety and tension. Indoor games and hobbies also take the pressure off your mind and are great stress relievers.*

# Doing meditation

***As Board exams were approaching, Sakshi felt more and more tense. She started experiencing frequent headaches and her backbone became stiff. She would complain of pain in her neck, shoulders and both the arms. Her mother took her to an orthopaedic doctor. He took some X-Rays, gave her some painkillers, and advised physiotherapy. When nothing worked, he referred her to a psychiatrist. The psychiatrist diagnosed the condition to be stress-related. He gave her some medicines and told her to practise meditation every day.***

*Meditation is a tool for Relaxation, Concentration and Enhancement.*

Stress and tension tend to diminish our brainpower. Unless stress is managed properly, there is no way to improve the functioning of the brain. Meditation is one of the best ways to manage stress. Meditation helps to make our mind calm. Calm mind, better retention power, sound health, focus and concentration are some of the key areas which are enhanced by meditation. Meditation also takes care of our mood problem.

**There are different types of meditation.**

- **Simple meditation** – the simplest form of meditation is, of course, focussing on breathing. Since your breath is always with you, it can be done anytime, anywhere. However, the best way is to settle down in a cool and quiet place and focus all your attention on your breathing.
- **Shabda meditation** – *Shabda* means sound. Focus your attention on the sounds you are able to hear. It can be a moving bus or the chugging of the train or your own breathing. Concentrate your entire attention on that sound. If your thoughts wander, bring them back and be aware of that particular sound only.

- ***Trataka* meditation** – this form of meditation involves focussing your vision on a particular object. Keep that object before you. Watch it for some time. Visualise it with closed eyes. Keep your thoughts on the vision of that object. When it goes away from your visualisation, bring it back and keep it in your consciousness. Apart from arresting the wavering mind, this type of meditation also improves the power of your brain by developing concentration, imagination, will-power and eyesight.

*The weak and idle mind cannot create powerful thoughts.*

- **Zen meditation** – practise this form of meditation in any comfortable and restful posture. Focus on your breathing. When some other thought intrudes, push it aside. While being attentive to the breathing process, start counting your breath with each exhalation. The total attention should be fixed on this one action of counting only.

Meditation has a relaxing effect on your body. Early mornings and just before going to bed are the best times to meditate. You can also do meditation before studying or eating.

When you try meditation, initially, you will find it difficult. But soon, you will gain command over it. Who knows you might end up as a Zen master or a spiritual guru and show the path of light to all.

# Listening to soothing music

***When Pooja's friend told her that the best way to practise Mathematics is by doing it with music on, she was exhilarated. It was like a dream come true. Pooja was very fond of the song 'Dus bahane kar ke le gaya dil.....' so she kept on listening to the song while doing her Maths exercises. When the song finished she would rewind it and play it over and over again. But this created a problem for her. After she had switched off her recorder, the song kept playing in her mind all the time. Even while she studied other subjects which required attention, her mind kept thinking of the song subconsciously.....***

*Music is the soul of life.*

This is a very common problem among students who combine studies and music. Music makes you feel good. But the kind of music you listen to, makes a big difference to your psyche. Not only the speed and pace of the music, but the presence or absence of lyrics also makes an impact on your subconscious mind. The best music for a student is slow and without lyrics. You can listen to Yanni, Kitaro and Beethoven. Plain instrumental music like Tibetan music of Nawang also has a calming effect.

Music is an important tool to improve and maintain brain functions. Music is very effective for concentration, memory skills and control of stress. Music affects your psychological state. When you are deeply involved in mental work, your pulse and blood pressure tend to rise. Your brain waves go up and the muscles get tensed up. Relaxation induced by specific music leaves the mind alert and able to concentrate. Baroque music is found to be most conducive to this state, reason being, most baroque music is timed at sixty beats per minute, which is the same as an average resting heart rate.

*The world is like a mirror. If you smile, it smiles at you, if you frown, it frowns back.*

Recent scientific development has created a new music variety called subliminal music. It is said to have coded signals that directly reach the subconscious mind. They give positive auto suggestions which improve your level of study.

Try these and see which one suits you best. Play your collection of soft music at times like study, eating and sleeping. It will have a natural, calming effect.

# Eating smart foods

**You must be wondering how food can be smart. There are certain foods that make you smart. We may call them smart foods. Smart foods are basically nutritious foods which help us think better.**

- The first group is **raw foods**. It is said that RAW is WAR against all ailments. Include in your diet all fruits and vegetables which can be eaten raw. Have fruits on an empty stomach. Taking fruits on an empty stomach helps in their easy digestion and hence, provides greater amount of energy. Did you know, two bananas can give enough energy to play a five-set tennis match? Also include salad with your daily meals. They provide you fibre, essential nutrients and prevent you from overeating.

*A healthy mind lives in a healthy body.*

- The second group is that of **the nut family**—almonds, cashews, pistachio, walnuts, hazel-nuts, peanuts. Nuts are rich in vitamins as well as protein. Apart from that, there are some vitamins like vitamin E and K, which are found in abundance in nuts.
- The third group is the **lentil group** which is rich in protein. You can have them soaked overnight. The live protein in these germinated seeds gives enormous nutrition and helps stay alert.
- The fourth and the most important group consists of **water**. Almost two-thirds of our body is made up of water. Drinking at least 10-12 glasses of water, daily, is essential. If you do not drink enough water, then you will feel lazy and sleepy. Constipation and headaches will become your constant companions. So keep some water on your study table and sip it every now and then, to remain alert.

*Nothing is so strong as gentleness, nothing so gentle as real strength.*

## Food for thought

One more important thing about eating is to have frequent small meals rather than eating two big meals which will instantly make you feel sleepy. Make sure you eat small quantities spaced out many times a day. This ensures that you won't doze off to sleep each time you nourish your body by eating a heavy meal.

*Here is a health food recipe for you.*

*Try it out and see how light and energetic you feel.*

### *Sprouts Bhel Puri*

## Ingredients

*1 cup sprouted moong/moth dal*

*½ cup murmura and sev*

*1 onion, 1 tomato, and ½ cucumber finely chopped*

*½ cup shredded carrot and cabbage*

*a little chopped coriander*

*juice of half a lemon*

*½ tsp chat masala*

*salt to taste*

## Method of Preparation

*Steam the sprouted dal lightly. Add all the ingredients. Mix it well and your healthy snack is ready.*

*Sprout bhel is healthy, fat-free and full of nutrients. You can take a bowlful of this dish and munch on it while studying. It makes a great snack.*

# Stretch your day

***You must be wondering what this is all about. Let me tell you about Raju, who was an active student with many hobbies, and engaged in extra-curricular activities. He was always short of time. He slept late and got up late too. He would wake up with a start and rush through all his chores in a hurry. Invariably, sometimes he would miss his school bus or leave his tiffin at home or forget to put on his school tie.... The list was endless. Having rushed through his morning hours, his mind would be set at a pace higher than normal which only made things worse. He had no time to relax. When his head hit the pillow at night, his mind would still be wandering around the chores left unattended. What a hectic life for someone who is barely 15 years old? It was not long before he suffered a burnout.***

*Begin your day at a leisurely pace for a calm and relaxed mind.*

If you are like Raju, if you are an active student with many co-curricular activities, you will definitely be short on time. You may be getting a big high out of your super efficient image by doing many things at the same time, but this will not go on for long. You need to slow down and give yourself time to relax.

The technique is very simple—wake up earlier than usual in the morning. Usually, a person who sleeps late, wakes up late too. A small change in your waking hours will make a big difference. Give yourself a breather in the form of an extra half an hour in the morning and see how relaxed you are the whole day. You will be amazed at your ability to perform all your activities with ease, and fit in everything smoothly in the same twenty-four hours which you had earlier too.

*Better by far you should forget and smile, than you should remember and be sad.*

I do not preach that you get up at this particular time or the early bird gets the worm. The simple solution lies in getting up earlier than whatever time you normally do. Basically, you start the day earlier.

What happens when you wake up early? It is really simple, actually. You get to start your day at a leisurely pace. It will make you feel your day stretched out before you. You will be calmer, less irritable and more relaxed when you do not have to begin your day rushing from one thing to another. At this moment, you need time for slowing down rather than sleeping those extra hours.

But before you start following this technique—a word of caution, the most important thing about getting up early is that you must not spend time in bed after you are awake. Just lingering in bed after waking up will drain out your energy and your mind will be tired in advance. Also, do not plead the person who is waking you up for some more time. Jump and spring up the moment you are awake and spend your entire day with renewed energy levels.

## Let's grill you

**Tick the right answer.**

***Marking key***

Give (1) mark for each 'a' answer and (2) marks for each 'b' answer.

**Marks**

1. In the morning, when your alarm goes off, you — a/b ☐
   a. put it off and go back to sleep.
   b. wake up instantly.
2. When someone comes to wake you up, you — a/b ☐
   a. plead for ten more minutes in bed.
   b. jump and spring out of bed.
3. When you assess your day on waking, you find the day is full and you have — a/b ☐
   a. very less time on hand.
   b. enough time to complete all the jobs.

4. To have some extra time in the day, you — a/b ☐
   a. give up one of the activities.
   b. wake up half an hour early.

5. You feel that to be an expert in time management, one — a/b ☐
   a. need not have fixed waking or sleeping hours.
   b. should be fairly regular in daily habits.

☐

### *Interpretation*

- **7 and above :** You know how to manage your time well. Waking up slightly early will help you relax.
- **6 and below :** Time management does not come naturally to you. It is a skill which you need to develop with the right attitude.

### *Just Chill*

Locate the acupressure point called "The great eliminator" on the fleshy bit between thumb and forefinger. Hold it with the thumb and forefinger of the other hand. Push in, squeeze slowly and firmly. It may feel tender, so hold and release until the tenderness disappears. The great eliminator is brilliant in times of stress, tension or just common headache.

# Examination Guide

Exams come in all shapes and sizes. As you excel in each class, the level of exams becomes tougher. Tests become exams which are held as quarterly, half-yearly and final exams. In higher classes, there are written exams, practical exams, viva voce, seminars, projects etc.

*It is very important to maintain balance between speed and accuracy in an exam.*

### Preparing for the exam

Usually, some preparatory leave is provided to the students before the exams. This is the time to revise all that you learnt throughout the year. Since these days are to be utilised totally for revising the syllabus, you need to reschedule your timetable.

- Display the examination date sheet at a prominent place.
- Check the syllabus of each subject.
- Keep textbooks and notes ready, subject-wise.
- Evaluate your own preparations as to whether you need extra effort in any subject.
- Reschedule your timetable in such a way that you alternate subjects to avoid boredom and have brief periods of rest and relaxation.

- Revise from your own notes.
- Browse through your textbooks for reference after reading your notes.
- Since exams have to be written, do include some writing everyday.
- Prepare those subjects first which do not have much gap before exam.
- Keep everything aside three days before the first exam and concentrate fully on the first paper.
- Stop the revision the evening before the exam.
- Do not forgo your sleep or allow tension to build up.
- Go to bed early.

**Last minute rush during Board exams**

- For your Board exam, you will be allotted a centre which will be any nearby school, other than your own school. Naturally, you would not be acquainted with it. Visit the school at least a day before the exams to avoid the last minute confusion.
- You must have been allotted your roll number much in advance. Have it laminated and keep at least two photocopies at home.
- The evening before the exam, keep your pens, pencils and other necessary items ready in your pencil box. Keep your roll number safely.
- If a water bottle is permitted, carry one with you. A few sips of water in between the exam are refreshing.
- On the day of the exam, wake up earlier than usual.
- Have a bath and get refreshed.
- If you want a quick revision, check your notes.
- Do nothing an hour or so before the exam.
- Stay calm. Breathe deeply to relax yourself.

*Man's height of glory is in the contribution he makes to serve others.*

# The next exam

When your first exam is over, revel in the fact that you have one subject less to study now. If you have time before the next exam, then use some time for relaxation. Take a walk, meet friends or watch your favourite soap on TV. Once you feel relaxed, begin revising for the next exam.

Keep this fact in mind that exams are only as far as they seem. Once they begin, they finish in a jiffy.

## WRITING THE EXAM

Among all types of exams like practical, viva voce, projects or seminar, the written exam requires maximum preparation as it carries maximum marks. There are two types of written examinations.

*You must be watchful. Let your whole life be in your own grip. Watch your own thoughts and keep your grip.*

### *1. SUBJECTIVE TYPE EXAMS*

These are the routine exams which test the student's overall performance. They include all sorts of questions.

- Recognition questions—to recognise instances and individuals.
- Recall questions—to test one's memory.
- Application questions—pertaining to practical application of knowledge.
- Analysis questions—they test a student's ability to analyse a particular situation.
- Synthesis questions—the ability to combine parts to form a whole answer.
- Evaluation questions—aim at evaluating a situation.

# Reading the questions properly

When students read the questions, it is a general tendency to spot the topic of the question and start writing. Students decide how well they know it. However, the important consideration should be what the examiner wants to know about the topic. Mark keywords in the question. Some of the typical key-words are—

- Explain in detail........
- Prove that...........
- What is your opinion about..........
- Discuss in detail...............
- How would you explain...........
- Write short notes on ......
- Briefly describe....
- Compare....with.......
- Describe......
- Give examples of .....
- Differentiate between......and .......

*Humility and silence carry great wisdom.*

These are some common ways of drafting questions. These are the little catches in the words that matter. Look for keywords and try to understand what the examiner really demands through this question. This is possible only when you read and understand the question correctly.

## Time management

- As you read through the question paper, plan your strategy. If you have any choice between the questions, then choose them carefully because if you do one option and later decide to attempt the other one, then you would be wasting your precious time.
- When we talk of time management, it does not mean that you have to divide your three hours or 180 minutes equally between your questions. You must consider their weightage and number of words you are to write for them. Accordingly, you may allot time for each question. A good strategy is to spend the initial ten minutes in noting down points for each question as you go through the paper, and forming a mental image of your answers.
- Now start writing the answers.
- Use your best handwriting.
- Use appropriate terms.
- Mind your spellings.
- Use correct punctuation marks.
- Write an attractive introduction.
- Follow it with the subject matter point-wise.
- Conclude with an emphatic ending.
- Keep an eye on the watch.
- Attempt all parts of the question.
- If you have to draw a diagram, do so within the timeframe you have allotted to that question.
- Recheck your answer paper after completion because careless mistakes account for loss of a lot of marks.

*The beauty of all things lies in your ability to appreciate them.*

*You are you. Enjoy being your real self.*

- Incorporate the corrections neatly.
- Only when you are convinced that you have put in your best effort in answering the question paper should you hand over the answer sheets.

### *TOO FAST*

Before we move on to the other type of paper, we would like to mention the problem of writing the answers **too fast**. Contrary to writing the answers too slowly, where you barely manage to finish the paper, is the problem of writing too fast. Some students try to write the answers as though they are in some sort of race. Writing fast is always at the cost of quality. No additional marks are given for being efficient and finishing the paper before time. Therefore, take your own time. If you have a few more minutes to spare, recheck the paper twice. Make sure you have not left out anything. Utilise this time because this is your last chance of making any changes before sealing your fate.

*Calmness and endurance increase your efficiency.*

### *2. OBJECTIVE TYPE EXAMS*

Objective type questions are common in competitive exams. It is generally a multiple choice question paper where four answers are given for each question. You need to tick the correct answer. Most students think that answering objective type questions is easy. They do not have to think of the answer, all they have to do is to choose the correct answer. However, this is not true. In such exams, simply memorising or cramming a lesson does not help. You not only need wider knowledge of that particular subject but of those as well which are linked with it. While choosing between the given answers, the fine distinction between the right answer and the nearly right answer requires one to understand the topic in depth.

### *How to attempt the objective type paper*

The best way to attempt these papers is to solve them in three rounds.

### *Round 1*

Before beginning the paper, read the instructions carefully. You must clearly understand if there are any choices. How many marks does each question carry? Is there any negative marking for wrong answer? Once you are clear about the instructions, answer all the questions you know for sure in the first round.

Also, tick those questions with a pencil which you can solve, but which need more time.

All this should not take more than 10-15 minutes.

### *Round 2*

In this round, answer those questions that you ticked with the pencil in the first round. Since they require some calculations, try to answer them as swiftly as you can.

This may take longer than the first round.

### *Round 3*

Finally get down to the most difficult questions. If there is no negative marking, then you can do some intelligent guessing. But do not attempt these questions if there is a risk of losing marks.

*Give others room to grow and they will stay with you.*

## Time management

Time is a very important constraint in objective type exams. You may be required to answer a hundred questions in an hour's time. That gives you 36 seconds to answer each question. Since you only need to tick a choice, 10 seconds are sufficient for reading and ticking a question if you know the answer. But when you are unsure of the answer, you should not waste time on it in the first round. Just mark it with a pencil. Try to solve such questions in the second round.

*The one who knows how to adjust, is the one who knows how to survive.*

Objective type exams are not easy, but they are not difficult either. The secret lies in getting enough practice in solving such questions within the time frame given. Also, you need to be thorough in your subject. Last minute study does not work for these exams. Boost up your knowledge by studying throughout the year. Obtain question papers of previous years and practise them.

**Remember, practice makes a man perfect.**

## A word of caution

When the exam is over, you come out and meet your friends. The temptation to compare answers and see how you have done overpowers you. But avoid this as far as possible. Once you have handed over the answer sheet, there is absolutely nothing that can be done. Making comparisons often causes confusion and doubt. This can be very discouraging at times and affects your performance in the next papers.

*A man with a bad temper is actually angry with himself.*

The best thing to do after the exam is to go home and relax for a while. Assess your personal performance and thank the Almighty for all that you have been able to achieve. Do not let negative thoughts take over and de-motivate you. What is done is behind you, but you still have to revise and prepare for your next exam. So put all your energies into it rather than brooding over the past.

# Career guide

Choosing a career is a tricky job. Having an insight into understanding how most students choose their careers is trickier than that. They all do it in different ways, depending upon their perspectives which developed with time.

*Remember, my child, you are very special No one can play your role better than you.*

Some pursue their 'I will grow up and be a doctor/ engineer/CA/......' dream. Some build on their aspirations of fame and fortune. There are some others who take up careers that come up during passionate discussions with friends and peers. Among them, the largest number is of those who are coerced into pursuing the career their parents have in mind for them.

Very rarely do we come across young adults whose career choices are based on sound information or a realistic understanding of what their chosen careers entail.

*When you smile, not only do you feel happy but you bring a ray of light into the lives of others.*

It is seldom that the consideration is 'What am I really good at?' or 'What do I enjoy doing most?'

Inevitably, after putting in several years of hard work, many find themselves nose deep in a job, but not a career. By the time the realisation dawns on them, it is a little too late!

Our purpose of writing this here is to help students make informed choices about careers, where it really counts—right at the beginning. This information will not only give you details about how to study right to excel in exams, but also enlighten you on the career facts and data. It also helps you to build up the dedication required to be in your favourite profession.

There are a multitude of careers coming up nowadays. We cannot cover them all in this limited space. However, we have tried to take up some of the latest and popular courses. A list of new courses is also given at the end to help you choose your favourite among them.

# Choosing a stream

As you already know, soon after class X, you have to choose your subjects according to your choice. This choice of subjects depends upon the career you wish to pursue later in life. Categorically, there are three streams offered in schools.

1. Science – Physics, Chemistry, Biology, Mathematics, Biotechnology, Computer Science
2. Commerce – Business Studies, Accountancy, Economics, Mathematics
3. Humanities – All the other subjects like History, Geography, English, Hindi, Sanskrit, etc. come under this category.

   - If you want to become an engineer, doctor, research scientist, architect, biotechnologist, pharmacist, you choose the Science stream.
   - For Commerce stream, there are many options open like CA, ICWA, ICSI, BBA, BCA, MBA.
   - Lecturership, Journalism, MBA, Law and various other fields are open for students opting for Humanities stream.
   - In fact, except for specialised studies like engineering, medicine, etc., all the fields are open for all the streams.

*A wise man is always anxious to learn, but never anxious to teach.*

These days, there are many new branches coming up which are innovative. Let's take a look at them.

*He, who has not learned, how to be gentle, loving and happy, has learned very little.*

### Actuarial Science

This science deals in analysis and modelling of problems in finance, risk management and product design in the areas of insurance, pensions, investment, banking and health care. Actuaries are invariably involved in the overall management of insurance companies and pension, gratuity and other employee benefit fund schemes. They provide professional services in a wide range of business and social contexts—

- Investment and financial services
- Life and health insurances
- General insurance
- Employee retirement and benefit plans

*One who conquers another is brave, but who conquers himself, is supremely noble.*

If you have attained 18 years of age and have passed 10+2 with atleast 85% marks in Mathematics, then you may be considered as student member of the Actuarial Society of India.

Website – www.actuariesindia.org

## Aeronautical/Aerospace Engineering

It pertains to designing, fabricating and operating all kinds of flying machines and related systems. Aeronautical engineers study subjects like aerodynamics, structures, propulsion, avionics etc. As an aeronautical engineer, you would be designing planes or doing research and development in this area.

Aerospace engineering includes more activities related to space like launching systems, satellites, communications and so on.

A 10+2 in Science with Mathematics can help you go into this field through an entrance test conducted by the institute.

Website – www.aaindore.com

*What we learn with pleasure, we never forget.*

## Alternative Medicines

While the Allopathic system of medicine (MBBS) has the largest number of followers in the world, there are other streams of medicine that have their own fan clubs. The most popular among these are Homoeopathy and Ayurveda, but there are others as well like Unani, Tibetan and so on.

After 10+2 in Physics, Chemistry and Biology, apply for the BAMS or BHMS degree to be an Ayurvedic doctor or Homeopathic doctor respectively.

Websites – www.ayurveda.com

www.abchomeopathy.com

### Animation

Animation industry in India is still in its infancy. However, it is not long before India captures the international market in this field also.

A 10+2 in any discipline is required to join a course in animation. An animator must have excellent creative and artistic abilities—a flair for drawing, sketching along with a good sense of humour and an observant eye to spot the incongruous. Numerous institutes have sprung up to turn you into a multimedia pro but a word of caution, don't just settle for any of the two bit courses offered at small time institutions. They won't get you anywhere.

*To be completely unaware is better than knowing the half-truth.*

Aptech University; BIT, Noida, FTII, Pune & NID, Ahmedabad offer recognised courses in animation.

www.arena-multimedia.com

### Architecture

Architecture is often misunderstood as a branch of engineering. This is definitely not so. Architects are the artists who help create a better world by designing better spaces with good view, fresh feel, inspiration and positive feelings.

After 10+2 with Physics, Chemistry and Maths, you need to take entrance tests for admission to an architecture college or an engineering college with architecture department. Engineering Drawing is a useful subject to take up at the 10+2 level if you are keen on architecture.

School of Planning and Architecture (SPA) in New Delhi is a premium institute for a course in architecture.

Website – www.spa.ernet.in

**Bioinformatics**

Bioinformatics is a new age discipline combining Biology and Information Technology (IT). It involves Computer Science and IT to handle biological information. Bioinformatics can be applied to all areas of life sciences including plant and animal sciences, energy, pharmacy and textiles.

You should have passed 10+2 in Science with Biology and Mathematics. There are many universities offering this course. JNU, New Delhi; Institute of Bioinformatics and Applied Biotechnology, Bangalore;and Bioinformatics Institute of India in Noida are a few among them.

Website – www.bii.com

*Only the weak fight. The strong rest on their strength and have no need to prove either to themselves or to others that they are strong.*

**Biotechnology**

Biotechnology is a fast emerging favourite among students because of its wide scope. Biotechnologists develop new and advanced pharmaceuticals, diagnostics and vaccines. They also work towards growing disease-resistant plants, vegetables and flowers with longer shelf life.

To pursue an undergraduate course in B.Tech. (Biotechnology), you should have Biology and Maths in 10+2. Although biotechnology is a field which has tremendous growth in the future, this is a field mainly for those who have a scientific bent of mind and who are inclined towards research.

AIIMS in New Delhi, and many other deemed universities like Jaypee Institute and Amity Institute also offer courses in Biotechnology.

Website – www.jiit.edu.in

## Hospital Management

It is the management of various activities taking place in the hospitals in a systematic manner just like management of hotels. It involves planning, execution, organisation, co-ordination, monitoring and evaluation. The major aspects covered under hospital management are—

- Health policy and administration
- Health planning
- Health economics
- Finance management
- Hospital planning

For more details, you may contact University of Delhi, Faculty of Management Studies, New Delhi.

website - www.fms.edu

*A thought constantly repeated becomes a habit.*

## Medical Laboratory Technology

Medical laboratory technologists work in pathological laboratories and conduct various tests and analyses on human blood, urine, stool and so on. They are also trained in operating various medical instruments like ECG, EEG.

To qualify as a laboratory technician, you need to do a degree in Medical laboratory technology after 10+2 in Science.

## Nutrition and Dietetics

The first picture that pops into mind when we talk of a dietician is that of someone who makes overweight people eat raw carrots for every meal until they have shed atleast 20 kilos. But this is not so. A dietician is much more than this. Every big hospital has trained dicticians as staff.

*Man is the maker of his happiness and fate.*

After doing 10+2 in Science, you can do an undergraduate course in Nutrition and Dietetics from Delhi University and the University of Pondicherry.

### Optometry

Optometrists are those who work at hospitals, clinics, nursing homes and contact lens manufacturing units. They are the ones who ask you to look into a hi-tech machine at an optician and declare whether you need spectacles or not.

After a 10+2 in Science, B.Sc. in optometry can be done from a good university.

### Physiotherapy

Physiotherapists work with people who have been disabled by accidents. People suffering from slipped discs, cervical spondylitis, fractures, body or facial paralysis or immobility of limbs due to illness use the services of physiotherapists. They also work with sportspersons to keep their muscles and joints in peak condition.

A degree in physiotherapy after 10+2 in Science enables you to run your own physiotherapy clinic.

*Life is full of difficulties. The difficulties which God sends us are few, but what we create for ourselves are plenty and without purpose.*

### Speech Therapy

Speech therapists work with the hearing impaired to teach them to speak and make themselves understood. They also work with people who have suffered strokes and other injuries to those parts of the brain that control speech and hearing. They also work with children who have speech defects like stammering.

After a 10+2 in Science, you may do this degree course.

### Textile Engineering

It is probably the softest of the various branches of engineering. The scope of textile engineering has expanded to non woven technology, polymer science and synthetic fibre production. Some textile engineers are even working with NASA to develop new materials for space suits.

Science with Maths in 10+2 is the right choice for those who wish to pursue this career.

National Institute of Fashion Technology (NIFT) in New Delhi has recently introduced a course in textile engineering.

Website – www.NIFT.com

Here is a comprehensive list of new courses which you can apply for, after completing 10+2 in respective streams.

*What worth is kingship without peace of mind.*

## Other Courses

Besides the traditional courses like MBBS, B.Tech., BCA, BBA etc, the following are some of the few career options which have recently come up. The list is endless and space limited. You may contact any of these websites and get information about your favourite career.

www.surfindia.com

www.careerlauncher.com

www.cetindia.com

www.careerguidance.com

www.uisb.edu

| Name of the course | University/ Institute | Qualifying exam |
|---|---|---|
| Actuarial Science<br>BA Insurance | • Delhi University | 10+2 in any stream |
| Fine Arts<br>BA | • College of Art,<br>New Delhi | 10+2 in any stream |
| Archaeology<br>BA (Archaeology) | • University of Baroda<br>• Bangalore University | 10+2 in any stream |
| Architecture<br>B.Arch. | School of Planning &<br>Architecture, New Delhi | 10+2 Physics, Chemistry<br>Maths, Engg. Drawing |
| Horticulture<br>B.Sc.(Hort) | • College of Agriculture,<br>Maharashtra<br>• College of Agriculture,<br>Andhra Pradesh | 10+2 PCB |
| Anthropology<br>B.Sc. | • Delhi University | 10+2 in any stream |
| Aquaculture<br>B.Sc. (Fisheries) | • College of Fisheries,<br>Kerala | 10+2 Science |
| Accessory design | • NIFT, New Delhi | 10+2 in any stream |
| BBA, BCA, BBS | • All state universities | 10+2 in any stream |
| Biotechnology<br>B.Sc.(Microbiology)<br>B.Tech. | • Delhi University<br>• Gurukul Kangri, U.P.<br>• All India Institute of<br>Medical Sciences,<br>New Delhi | 10+2 PCMB |
| Journalism<br>B.A.(Mass Com) | • Delhi University<br>• Bombay University<br>• Institute of Mass<br>Communication,<br>New Delhi<br>• Jamia Millia University,<br>New Delhi | 10+2 in any stream |

| Printing and Publishing B.A. (Book publishing, editing, sales) | • Delhi University | 10+2 in any stream |
|---|---|---|
| Photography Integrated degree course in Photography | • University of Pune | 10+2 in any stream |
| Social Work BSW | • Jamia Millia University, New Delhi | 10+2 in any stream |

**Some other courses include—**

- Visual Art
- Computer Graphics
- Library Science
- Travel & Tourism
- Cost Accountancy
- Nanotechnology
- Forensic Science
- Counselling Psychology
- Civil Aviation
- Air Hostess
- Commercial Pilot
- Chartered Accountancy
- Company Secretary
- Nanoscience
- Disaster Management
- Networking Technology

# Miles to go...

The personality of an individual is determined by his attitude, his prerogatives, his perceptions and his priorities in life. Once you have set definite goals, you must understand how the learning process works and also where you stand in achieving these goals. Adopting good study habits effectively is a sure way of achieving success. Once you have tasted success in life, even if it is in a small quantity, your heart will be filled with a feeling of accomplishment. It is a nice feeling which brings you immense joy. You wish it could last forever. This is the time when you feel closest to your own self. Be true to yourself. You have just begun the journey of life. You need to gear up for greater challenges.

Aim for the moon and even if you miss it, you will land among the stars. Target the best ranks in your school. As you move ahead, you will find that different tools work at different times. Like a true warrior you must know what works when. It helps you choose the right technique at the right moment.

*I believe that God is in me as the sun is in the colour and fragrance of a flower—the light in my darkness—the voice in my silence.*

Once you have studies under your control, you can focus on other areas in life. Remember, life is not all about studies. There is much more to it. Friends and family form an integral part of your life. The success that you attain in studies will gradually creep into all the areas in your life. Soon you will realise that you become more receptive of changes and have disciplined your mind. What began as a path leading to success in exams became your path towards achievement in life. Now you can go anywhere you want and success will follow you. Dare to dream big and remain true to your own self. You will soon be shaking hands with success.

And remember, it is just the beginning,

....there are miles to go before you sleep.

# Career & Management

168 pp • Rs. 120/-

160 pp • Rs. 80/-
Also available in Hindi

144 pp • Rs. 80/-

172 pp • Rs. 125/-

136 pp • Rs. 96/-

128 pp • Rs. 96/-

100 pp • Rs. 150/-

144 pp • Rs. 96/-

128 pp • Rs. 80/-

120 pp • Rs. 80/-

184 pp • Rs. 88/-

160 pp • Rs. 95/-

200 pp • Rs. 88/-

200 pp • Rs. 96/-

106 pp • Rs. 80/-

248 pp • Rs. 150/-

132 pp • Rs. 120/-

192 pp • Rs. 150/-

128 pp • Rs. 96/-

120 pp • Rs. 75/-
Earlier printed as
Teens to Twenties

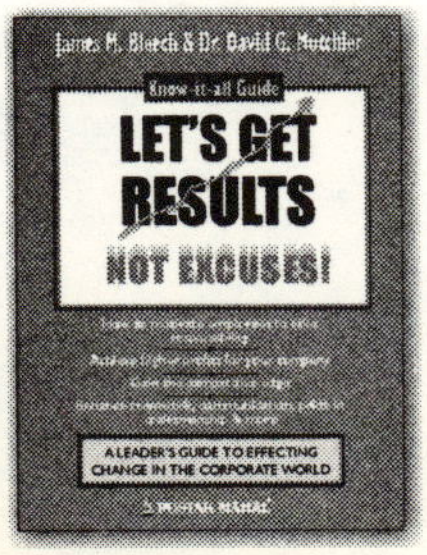


240 pp • Rs. 195/-

176 pp • Rs. 150/-

96 pp • Rs. 96/-

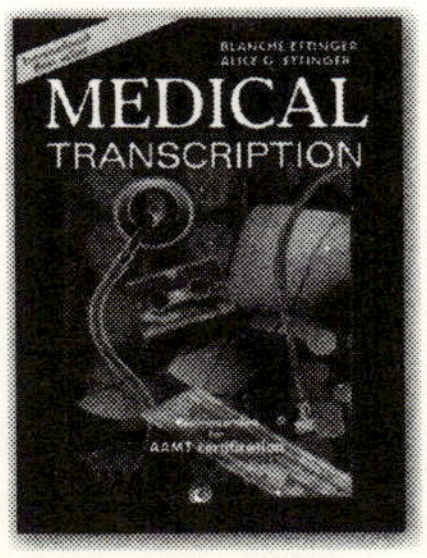


472 pp • Rs. 450/-

280 pp • Rs. 175/-